GUIDE TO

MARTIN'S
ANNUAL CRIMINAL CODE

Owen Haw, B.A., LL.B., LL.M.

In cooperation with
Canada Law Book Inc.
publisher of

MARTIN'S ANNUAL CRIMINAL CODE
by
Edward L. Greenspan, Q.C.
and
The Honourable Mr. Justice Marc Rosenberg

2004

EMOND MONTGOMERY PUBLICATIONS LTD.
TORONTO, CANADA

Printed in Canada.

Edited, designed, and typeset by WordsWorth Communications, Toronto.

We acknowledge the financial support of the Government of Canada through the Book Publishing Industry Development Program (BPIDP) for our publishing activities.

Library and Archives Canada Cataloguing in Publication

Haw, Owen
    Guide to Martin's annual criminal code / Owen Haw.

"In cooperation with Canada Law Book Inc. publisher of Martin's Annual Criminal Code by Edward L. Greenspan, Q.C. and The Honourable Mr. Justice Marc Rosenberg".
ISBN 1-55239-142-6

    1. Criminal law—Canada—Textbooks.   2. Canada. Criminal Code.
I. Title.   II. Title: Martin's annual criminal code.

KE8809.H39 2004   345.71   C2004-904695-0
KF9220.ZA2H39 2004

Table of Contents

Preface

Martin's Annual Criminal Code contains a wealth of information concisely packaged in one book. The challenge lies in quickly and easily retrieving the information you need.

This *Guide to Martin's Annual Criminal Code* was created to help students gain mastery of the skills and knowledge that enable full and effective use of Martin's. Written in plain language and with easy-to-understand directions, the guide explains and demonstrates how to use specific features of Martin's, such as the Annotations, the Criminal Code Concordance and the Offence Grid, and how to correctly fill out forms, such as an information.

Many examples relevant to law enforcement are provided to show where and how information can be found. Pages from Martin's are reproduced with the examples, so that students can immediately see what is being explained, without having to leaf through Martin's itself.

Approximately 50 exercises have also been included in the guide to lead students to the next learning step — doing it for themselves.

1 Introduction to Martin's

The first time you start looking through *Martin's Annual Criminal Code*, it may appear confusing and difficult to use because of the large quantity of information arranged in so many different sections.

However, the more familiar you become with it, the more you will appreciate having so much information available in one book. Martin's provides a first step for analyzing any criminal law matter, be it procedural or substantive. Often the information will be sufficiently comprehensive that there will be no need to look further.

This study guide is intended to help you learn how to find what you need quickly and with ease, and to fully benefit from the breadth and depth of information within Martin's.

Most of Martin's consists of the *Criminal Code*, reproduced in full, and extensive commentary immediately following each section of the Code. The commentary, which is divided into three segments (Cross-References, Synopsis and Annotations), is researched and written by lawyers expert in criminal law, and it is where much of the value of Martin's lies. This is what makes Martin's different from the *Criminal Code* published by the Government of Canada, which you can find on the Internet.

In addition to the *Criminal Code*, R.S.C. 1985, c. C-46, other selected federal statutes, such as the *Canada Evidence Act*, the *Controlled Drugs and Substances Act* and the *Youth Criminal Justice Act*, are included with Annotations. (Cross-References and Synopsis are included with the *Criminal Code* only.) These statutes are commonly used in the practice of criminal law and are convenient to have at your fingertips. Further important statutes can be found in a similar format in *Martin's Related Criminal Statutes*.

There are other features, such as the *Criminal Code* Concordance and the Offence Grid, that provide valuable information when you learn how to use them. These will be described later.

2 Table of Contents and Page Numbering

To get a general sense of what is included in Martin's, take a look at the Table of Contents, which lists the statutes, tables and other features in the order they appear in the book and provides page references.

Note that the page numbering does not run consecutively from the beginning to the end of the book. Instead, the book is divided into segments and the page numbering for each segment starts at "1". An abbreviation is used to distinguish the segments and the page numbers that apply to each. For example, the largest part of Martin's is the *Criminal Code,* and the abbreviation for this segment is "CC". There are over 1,500 pages covering the *Criminal Code,* starting with CC/1.

No longer applicable 2007 edition

The abbreviations used are fairly obvious and not difficult to remember. They are listed below.

Table of Contents	C	✓
Preface	P	✓
Criminal Code Concordance	CON	✓
Table of Cases	TC	✓
Criminal Code	CC	N/a – PG 1 – 1630
Canada Evidence Act	CE	N/a – PG 1631 – 1700
Charter of Rights	CH	N/a – PC 1701 – 1774
Controlled Drugs and Substances Act	CD	N/A – PG 1775 – 1829
Crimes Against Humanity and War Crimes Act	WC	N/a – PG 1831 – 1844
Youth Criminal Justice Act	YC	N/a – PG 1851 – 1955
Offence Grid	OG	✓
Index	IN	✓
Appendix/Forms of Charges	A	✓

Page numbers are shown at the bottom of the page, with the abbreviation first and then the number (*e.g.*, CC/535).

Example 2.1

Your professor is discussing a defence of mental disorder under s. 16 of the *Criminal Code*, and tells you that helpful court interpretations of the word "wrong" can be found on page CC/54 of Martin's (reproduced on page 5). When you turn to page 54 in the *Criminal Code* portion of the text (CC), you will find a paragraph heading for "Meaning of 'wrong'", followed by a short discussion of court decisions that are important in deciding this question.

Example 2.2

Your professor then discusses how the *Canadian Charter of Rights and Freedoms* imposes the principles of fundamental justice upon Canadian criminal law and suggests that you look on page CH/11 of Martin's (reproduced on page 6). On page 11 of the Charter segment (CH), you will find s. 7 of the Charter set out — the section that incorporates principles of fundamental justice into the Constitution.

Once you learn the abbreviations, you will be able to quickly find your way through the text.

Exercises

2.1 What is on page TC/1?

TABLE OF CASES

2.2 What is on page C/1?

TABLE OF CONTENTS

2.3 What is on page YC/4?

DECLARATION OF PRINCIPLE

In *R. v. Wolfson*, [1965] 3 C.C.C. 304, 46 C.R. 8 (Alta. S.C. App. Div.), it was held that evidence of an irresistible impulse is not, by itself, enough to support a finding of insanity under this section.

Meaning of "wrong" – The term "wrong" in subsec. (2) means "morally wrong" and not simply "legally wrong". The court must determine whether the accused, because of a disease of the mind, was rendered incapable of knowing that the act committed was something that he ought not to have done. Thus, the inquiry cannot terminate with the discovery that the accused knew that the act was contrary to the formal law. A person may know that the act was contrary to law and yet, by reason of a disease of the mind, be incapable of knowing that the act is morally wrong in the circumstances according to the moral standards of society: *R. v. Chaulk*, [1990] 3 S.C.R. 1303, 62 C.C.C. (3d) 193, 2 C.R. (4th) 1.

Example 2.1 Interpretation by courts

The inquiry under this section focuses not on a general capacity to know right from wrong, but rather on the ability to know that a particular act was wrong in the cirumstances. The accused must not only possess the intellectual ability to know right from wrong in an abstract sense but must possess the ability to apply that knowledge in a rational way to the alleged criminal act. The crux of the inquiry is whether the accused lacks the capacity to rationally decide whether the act is right or wrong and hence to make a rational choice of whether to do it or not. The accused would not be criminally responsible where, by reason of delusions, he perceives an act which is wrong as right or justifiable, and the disordered condition of his mind deprives the accused of the ability to rationally evaluate what he is doing. It is not necessary to show that, if the delusions were true, a specific defence such as self-defence would also apply: *R. v. Oommen*, [1994] 2 S.C.R. 507, 91 C.C.C. (3d) 8, 30 C.R. (4th) 195.

Mental illness short of insanity – Our *Criminal Code* does not recognize the defence of diminished responsibility and even though the accused may have been ill at the time of the offence he is technically sane if he was able to distinguish between right and wrong: *R. v. Chartrand*, [1977] 1 S.C.R. 314, 26 C.C.C. (2d) 417, 64 D.L.R. (3d) 145 (8:0).

Nevertheless where the accused is charged with an offence which requires proof of a specific intent, evidence that the accused was suffering from mental illness or mental disorder, though falling short of proof of insanity, may negative the requisite specific intent, as in the case of murder reduce the charge to manslaughter: *R. v. Baltzer, supra*. And to the same effect: *R. v. Hilton* (1977), 34 C.C.C. (2d) 206 (Ont. C.A.); *R. v. Meloche* (1975), 34 C.C.C. (2d) 184 (Que. C.A.); *R. v. Lechasseur* (1977), 38 C.C.C. (2d) 319 (Que. C.A.); *R. v. Browning* (1976), 34 C.C.C. (2d) 200 (Ont. C.A.); *R. v. Leblanc* (1991), 4 C.R. (4th) 98, [1991] R.J.Q. 686 (C.A.); *R. v. Wright* (1979), 48 C.C.C. (2d) 334, 11 C.R. (3d) 257 (Alta. S.C. App. Div.), leave to appeal to S.C.C. refused 48 C.C.C. (2d) 334n; *R. v. Bailey* (1996), 111 C.C.C. (3d) 122, 133 W.A.C. 105 (B.C.C.A.).

Where evidence is adduced in support of a defence of insanity to a charge of first degree murder, the jury is to be directed to first consider that defence. If that defence fails, then the jury should consider all the evidence in the case, including relevant evidence which was adduced in support of the insanity defence to determine whether the accused had the relevant intent for murder and, if so, whether the killing was planned and deliberate: *R. v. Allard* (1990), 57 C.C.C. (3d) 397, 78 C.R. (3d) 228, [1990] R.J.Q. 1847 (C.A.).

Procedure – Where the accused seeks to introduce evidence to support a defence of automatism, whether insane or non-insane automatism, a *voir dire* should not be resorted to where the evidence is relevant and not subject to rejection on any recognized legal ground. The evidence should be led before the jury and at the end of the case it will be for the trial judge to instruct the jury whether there is any evidence which will support the particular defence: *R. v. Sproule* (1975), 26 C.C.C. (2d) 92, 30 C.R.N.S. 56 (Ont. C.A.).

The accused may raise the defence of insanity at any time during the trial and in fact may raise the defence after the trier of fact has found the accused guilty but prior to conviction. If, during the course of the trial, prior to the finding of guilt, evidence is led which does not satisfy the trier of fact of insanity under this section, such evidence may nevertheless be

CC / 54

United States of America (1994), 93 C.C.C. (3d) 500, 119 D.L.R. (4th) 333, 84 W.A.C. 1 (B.C.C.A.), *per* Taylor J.A., affd for the reasons of Taylor J.A., [1996] 1 S.C.R. 469, 104 C.C.C. (3d) 446, 132 D.L.R. (4th) 383.

An extradition judge has no jurisdiction to grant Charter remedies with respect to violations of s. 6 as mobility rights are not engaged at the committal stage. The extradition judge does, however, have the discretion to hear evidence relating to an allegation that mobility rights will be subsequently violated at the ministerial stage by the fugitive's surrender. In considering whether to hear evidence in respect of the Charter breach, the extradition judge must have regard to the need for the expeditious disposition of the issue of committal, the danger of confusion from the reception of irrelevant evidence and waste that will result if the Minister ultimately declines the surrender: *United States of America v. Kwok*, [2001] 1 S.C.R. 532, 152 C.C.C. (3d) 225, 41 C.R. (5th) 44.

Legal Rights

**Example 2.2
What the section says**

LIFE, LIBERTY AND SECURITY OF PERSON.

7. Everyone has the right to life, liberty and security of the person and the right not to be deprived thereof except in accordance with the principles of fundamental justice.

ANNOTATIONS

Interpretation – The phrase "principles of fundamental justice" does not describe a protected right itself but rather qualifies the protected right not to be deprived of life, liberty and security of the person. The meaning of the principles of fundamental justice was to be determined having regard to the purpose of the section and its context in the Charter. Thus ss. 8 to 14 of the Charter address specific deprivations of the right to life, liberty and security of the person in breach of the principles of fundamental justice, and as such, violations of this section. They are designed to protect, in a specific manner and setting, the right to life, liberty and security of the person. The term "fundamental justice" was not synonymous merely with natural justice. The principles of fundamental justice are to be found in the basic tenets and principles not only of our judicial process, but also of the other components of the legal system. While many of the principles of fundamental justice are procedural in nature, they are not limited solely to procedural guarantees. Whether any given principle might be said to be a principle of fundamental justice within the meaning of this section will rest upon an analysis of the nature, sources, rationale and essential role of that principle within the judicial process and in the legal system as it evolves: *Reference re Section 94(2) of the Motor Vehicle*, [1985] 2 S.C.R. 486, 23 C.C.C. (3d) 289, 48 C.R. (3d) 289.

The harm principle is not a principle of fundamental justice. While the presence of harm to others may justify legislative action under the criminal law power, the absence of proven harm does not create an unqualified barrier to legislative action. The state may be justified in criminalizing conduct that is either not harmful or harmful only to the accused. The relevant principle of fundamental justice is that the parliamentary response must not be grossly disproportionate to the state interest sought to be protected. The criminalization of the possession of marijuana does not violate the principles of fundamental justice: *R. v. Malmo-Levine; R. v. Caine* (2003), 179 C.C.C. (3d) 417, 233 D.L.R. (4th) 415 (S.C.C.).

It was not open to a witness, the former manager of a bank in the Bahamas, to allege an infringement of his rights under s. 7 because he was required to testify in Canada about affairs in the Bahamas, in possible violation of Bahamian legislation. Any infringement of the witness's liberty or security did not result from the operation of Canadian law but solely from the operation of Bahamian law in the Bahamas: *R. v. Spencer*, [1985] 2 S.C.R. 278, 21 C.C.C. (3d) 385, 21 D.L.R. (4th) 756.

Section 7 does not apply retrospectively and thus an accused charged with an offence allegedly committed prior to the proclamation of the Charter cannot argue that the provision violated his rights as guaranteed by this section because in effect it imposed absolute liability

The Criminal Code

ORGANIZATION

Introduction

The *Criminal Code* is a large federal statute with over 1,000 sections and more than 60 forms. It sets out the many different offences that constitute criminal activity in Canada and outlines the procedures for processing cases. The sections and forms are organized by topic and divided into 34 Parts. All the forms are in the last Part.

Numbering System

You need to be familiar with the numbering system of the Code in order to quickly locate the information you are looking for.

Parts are numbered primarily by Roman numerals — for example, Part XII / Offences Relating to Currency. Some Parts have a Roman numeral followed by a decimal point and a standard number — for example, Part XII.1 / Instruments and Literature for Illicit Drug Use. This form of numbering indicates that, at some point, there was a legislative amendment (a change to the Code that was passed by Parliament) that inserted Part XII.1 into the existing Code. (For further information on amendments and their effects on numbering, see Chapter 5 of this study guide.)

Sections are numbered with standard numerals (*e.g.*, s. 16). When an amendment adds a new section or subsection that relates to or expands upon the subject-matter of an existing section or subsection, the new provision has the same number as the existing provision with a decimal point and a number added.

 Example 3.1

Look at ss. 249 and 249.1 (reproduced on page 8). Section 249.1 was added after s. 249 and is clearly related to it. Notice that subsec. 249.1(3) refers specifically to a provision of s. 249 in describing the circumstances in which the offence occurs.

Motor Vehicles, Vessels and Aircraft

DANGEROUS OPERATION OF MOTOR VEHICLES, VESSELS AND AIRCRAFT /
Punishment / Dangerous operation causing bodily harm / Dangerous operation
causing death.

Example 3.1
The first of two
related provisions

249. (1) Every one commits an offence who operates

(*a*) a motor vehicle in a manner that is dangerous to the public, having regard to all the circumstances, including the nature, condition and use of the place at which the motor vehicle is being operated and the amount of traffic that at the time is or might reasonably be expected to be at that place;

(*b*) a vessel or any water skis, surf-board, water sled or other towed object on or over any of the internal waters of Canada or the territorial sea of Canada, in a manner that is dangerous to the public, having regard to all the circumstances, including the nature and condition of those waters or sea and the use that at the time is or might reasonably be expected to be made of those waters or sea;

(*c*) an aircraft in a manner that is dangerous to the public, having regard to all the circumstances, including the nature and condition of that aircraft or the place or air space in or through which the aircraft is operated; or

(*d*) railway equipment in a manner that is dangerous to the public, having regard to all the circumstances, including the nature and condition of the equipment or the place in or through which the equipment is operated.

(2) Every one who commits an offence under subsection (1)

(*a*) is guilty of an indictable offence and liable to imprisonment for a term not exceeding five years; or

(*b*) is guilty of an offence punishable on summary conviction.

(3) Every one who commits an offence under subsection (1) and thereby causes bodily harm to any other person is guilty of an indictable offence and liable to imprisonment for a term not exceeding ten years.

(4) Every one who commits an offence under subsection (1) and thereby causes the death of any other person is guilty of an indictable offence and liable to imprisonment for a term not exceeding fourteen years. R.S.C. 1985, c. 27 (1st Supp.), s. 36; c. 32 (4th Supp.), s. 57; 1994, c. 44, s. 11.

FLIGHT / Punishment / Flight causing bodily harm or death / Punishment.

Example 3.1
A later provision
related to s. 249

249.1 (1) Every one commits an offence who, operating a motor vehicle while being pursued by a peace officer operating a motor vehicle, fails, without reasonable excuse and in order to evade the peace officer, to stop the vehicle as soon as is reasonable in the circumstances.

(2) Every one who commits an offence under subsection (1)

(*a*) is guilty of an indictable offence and liable to imprisonment for a term not exceeding five years; or

(*b*) is guilty of an offence punishable on summary conviction.

(3) Every one commits an offence who causes bodily harm to or the death of another person by operating a motor vehicle in a manner described in paragraph 249(1)(*a*), if the person operating the motor vehicle was being pursued by a peace officer operating a motor vehicle and failed, without reasonable excuse and in order to evade the police officer, to stop the vehicle as soon as is reasonable in the circumstances.

(4) Every person who commits an offence under subsection (3)

(*a*) if bodily harm was caused, is guilty of an indictable offence and liable to imprisonment for a term not exceeding 14 years; and

(*b*) if death was caused, is guilty of an indictable offence and liable to imprisonment for life. 2000, c. 2, s. 1.

Forms are numbered in a similar way. New forms that are created as a result of an amendment to a section are numbered like new sections — for example, Form 5.1.

Martin's makes it easy to find a particular section or form in the *Criminal Code* by indicating at the top of the page the number of the section or form set out or discussed on that page.

Parts, Topic Categories and Sections

Generally, offences created by the *Criminal Code* are set out in Parts II through XIII. Parts XIV through XXVIII deal with the procedural aspects of criminal law, such as preliminary inquiries (Part XVIII) and summary convictions (Part XXVII).

Each Part of the Code groups the provisions relating to particular categories of offences or procedures according to their common characteristics. These topic categories are identified by headings within each Part, which are listed in the Table of Contents, in order of appearance, under the Part heading.

 Example 3.2

Look at Part IX / Offences Against Rights of Property in the Table of Contents (reproduced below). These topic categories are important guides when you want to locate the provisions relating to a particular offence.

PART IX / OFFENCES AGAINST RIGHTS OF PROPERTY CC/605
    Interpretation
    Theft
    Offences Resembling Theft
    Robbery and Extortion
    Criminal Interest Rate
    Breaking and Entering
    Having in Possession
    False Pretences
    Forgery and Offences Resembling Forgery

**Example 3.2
Topic categories:
aids to finding
sections in the Code**

Example 3.3

Part VIII / Offences Against the Person and Reputation consists of the offences that cause injury, death or some form of physical or psychological trauma to a person. The chart on page 10 lists several of the many topic categories in Part VIII and some of the sections found under these headings, along with the subject-matter identified in the Code for each section.

**Example 3.3
Some of the
topic categories
and sections
found in Part VIII**

Murder, Manslaughter and Infanticide

    Murder, s. 229

    Murder Reduced to Manslaughter, s. 232

    Punishment for Murder, s. 235

Motor Vehicles, Vessels and Aircraft

    Dangerous Operation of Motor Vehicles, Vessels and Aircraft, s. 249

    Failure to Stop at Scene of Accident, s. 252

    Warrants to Obtain Blood Samples, s. 256

Assaults

    Assault with a Weapon Causing Bodily Harm, s. 267

    Disarming a Peace Officer, s. 270.1

    Sexual Assault, s. 271

Hate Propaganda

    Advocating Genocide, s. 318

    Public Incitement of Hatred, s. 319

Exercises

3.1 What Part of the *Criminal Code* deals with sexual offences? (Hint: use the Table of Contents.)

    Part V (5)

3.2 What section number is noted at the top corner of the first page of the sexual offences Part?

    150.1

3.3 What is noted at the bottom corner?

    Sec 275

DEFINITIONS

The *Criminal Code* does not begin with Part I; there are four sections that precede it: s. 1, Short Title, and three sections grouped under the heading Interpretation — s. 2, Definitions; s. 3, Descriptive Cross-References; and s. 3.1, Effect of Judicial Acts.

Section 2 is of particular interest, because it sets out the definitions that apply to the entire Code. The first words of s. 2 are "In this Act", and the definitions then follow. Therefore, every word or phrase defined in s. 2 has that same meaning throughout the Code.

In contrast, definitions found elsewhere in the Code apply only to the particular Part or sections to which they refer, not to the entire Code.

If you need a definition for a word that is not defined in the *Criminal Code* at all, you can refer to related statutes or to a dictionary.

Example 3.4

If you turn to s. 118 of the *Criminal Code* (reproduced on page 12), you will see that it is the first section in Part IV / Offences Against the Administration of Law and Justice. The first words of the section are "In this Part", followed by definitions of several words and phrases. The application of these definitions is limited to Part IV only.

Look at the Cross-References text for s. 118. This commentary indicates that it is necessary to refer back to s. 2 for the definitions of certain other words and phrases that are used in Part IV.

It is important to understand which definitions apply only to the individual Part (or to one or more sections within a Part) — those set out within the Part — and which definitions apply to the entire Code — those set out in s. 2.

Some words are defined both in s. 2 and in other sections of the *Criminal Code*. If there are conflicting definitions, which one applies?

Example 3.5

The word "weapon" is defined in both s. 2 and subsec. (2) of s. 270.1, Disarming a Peace Officer. A careful reading of the two definitions shows that the definition of "weapon" in subsec. 270.1(2) is more specific and more restrictive than the s. 2 definition.

The broader s. 2 definition includes "any thing used, designed to be used or intended for use (*a*) in causing death or injury . . . or (*b*) for the purpose of threatening or intimidating. . . ."

The narrower subsec. 270.1(2) definition requires that to be a weapon, the thing must be "designed to be used to cause injury or death to, or to temporarily incapacitate. . . ."

Where there is a conflict between the two definitions, the subsec. 270.1(2) definition applies to s. 270.1 and the offence it creates.

Example 3.4
Application of
definitions

Part IV / OFFENCES AGAINST THE ADMINISTRATION OF LAW AND JUSTICE

Interpretation

DEFINITIONS / "Evidence" or "statement" / "Government" / "Judicial proceeding" / "Office" / "Official" / "Witness".

118. In this Part

"evidence" or "statement" means an assertion of fact, opinion, belief or knowledge, whether material or not and whether admissible or not;

"government" means
    (*a*) the Government of Canada,
    (*b*) the government of a province, or
    (*c*) Her Majesty in right of Canada or a province;

"judicial proceeding" means a proceeding
    (*a*) in or under the authority of a court of justice,
    (*b*) before the Senate or House of Commons or a committee of the Senate or House of Commons, or before a legislative council, legislative assembly or house of assembly or a committee thereof that is authorized by law to administer an oath,
    (*c*) before a court, judge, justice, provincial court judge or coroner,
    (*d*) before an arbitrator or umpire, or a person or body of persons authorized by law to make an inquiry and take evidence therein under oath, or
    (*e*) before a tribunal by which a legal right or legal liability may be established,
whether or not the proceeding is invalid for want of jurisdiction or for any other reason;

"office" includes
    (*a*) an office or appointment under the government,
    (*b*) a civil or military commission, and
    (*c*) a position or an employment in a public department;

"official" means a person who
    (*a*) holds an office, or
    (*b*) is appointed to discharge a public duty;

"witness" means a person who gives evidence orally under oath or by affidavit in a judicial proceeding, whether or not he is competent to be a witness, and includes a child of tender years who gives evidence but does not give it under oath, because, in the opinion of the person presiding, the child does not understand the nature of an oath. R.S., c. C-34, s. 107; R.S.C. 1985, c. 27 (1st Supp.), s. 15.

CROSS-REFERENCES

In addition to the definitions set out in this section, applicable to offences created by this Part, reference should also be made to s. 2 and in particular the definitions of "justice", "provincial court judge", "peace officer", "public department", "public officer" and "Attorney General".

Other relevant definitions

3.4 When working with s. 177, Trespassing at Night, you will need to understand the meaning of "prowls by night". What is the definition of "night"?

_____

_____

_____

_____

_____

3.5 Where and how does the *Criminal Code* define "theft", "steal" and "robbery"? (Hint: use the Index.)

_____

_____

_____

_____

_____

3.6 When working with s. 348, Breaking and Entering . . . , you will need to understand the meaning of "breaking", "entering" and "place". Where are the definitions for these terms? (Hint: use the Index.)

_____

_____

_____

_____

_____

4 Commentary: Cross-References, Synopsis and Annotations

INTRODUCTION

Following almost every section of *Martin's Annual Criminal Code* is a commentary organized under three main headings: Cross-References; Synopsis; and Annotations. Note that the commentary on other statutes included in Martin's is limited to Annotations; there are no Cross-References or Synopsis.

The commentary, which has been written by leading criminal lawyers, is what distinguishes Martin's from a bare-bones *Criminal Code* as published by the Government of Canada. It is here that you will find much of the value of Martin's to students and other readers. The information provided in the commentary will help you to understand the meaning of each section of the *Criminal Code* and how it has been interpreted and applied by the courts.

CROSS-REFERENCES

The Cross-References identify sections of related statutes or other sections within the *Criminal Code* that have an impact on the particular section being examined. For example, under Cross-References for s. 92, the offence of Possession of Firearm Knowing Its Possession Is Unauthorized, reference is made to sections of the *Firearms Act*.

The *Canadian Charter of Rights and Freedoms* and the *Interpretation Act*, R.S.C. 1985, c. I-21, are also sometimes cross-referenced.

Example 4.1

Look at s. 12, Offence Punishable Under More Than One Act (reproduced below). This section prohibits punishing a person under more than one statute for the same offence, and it is significant where a charge could be laid under more than one statute. For example, if a person breaks into a doctor's office, steals morphine tablets and is caught leaving the building because a silent alarm has alerted the police, a charge of breaking and entering and committing theft under ss. 348 and 334 of the *Criminal Code* may be laid, and a charge of having unlawful possession of a Schedule I substance contrary to s. 4 of the *Controlled Drugs and Substances Act* also may be laid.

The Cross-References following s. 12 identify a number of related sections within the *Criminal Code* and in the Charter that will assist in the determination of whether this section applies in a particular case. The reader is directed to sources for further research, and considerable time may be saved that would otherwise have been spent researching other Parts of the Code and other statutes.

Example 4.1
Related sections and
other sources

OFFENCE PUNISHABLE UNDER MORE THAN ONE ACT.

12. Where an act or omission is an offence under more than one Act of Parliament, whether punishable by indictment or on summary conviction, a person who does the act or makes the omission is, unless a contrary intention appears, subject to proceedings under any of those Acts, but is not liable to be punished more than once for the same offence. R.S., c. C-34, s. 11.

CROSS-REFERENCES

As to an *autrefois* plea, see ss. 7(6), 607 to 610 of the Code and s. 11(*h*) of the *Charter of Rights and Freedoms*. As to the abuse of process generally, see notes following s. 579. As to the common law rule precluding multiple convictions for same *delict*, the "*Kienapple*" rule and common law principles of *res judicata* and issue estoppel, see notes following s. 613.

The Cross-References will identify additional relevant definitions, which may be found elsewhere in the *Criminal Code*, such as s. 2 (the definitions section), or in other statutes or important cases.

Example 4.2

Look at the Cross-References under s. 119, Bribery of Judicial Officers, Etc. / Consent of Attorney General (reproduced on page 17).

You will be directed to definitions of words used in s. 119, such as "office" and "corruptly". The Cross-References tell you that "office" is defined in

s. 118. "Corruptly" is not defined in this Part of the Code; instead, the Cross-References paraphrase the meaning set out by the court in *R. v. Brown* (1956), 116 C.C.C. 287 (Ont. C.A.).

Corruption and Disobedience

BRIBERY OF JUDICIAL OFFICERS, ETC. / Consent of Attorney General.

119. (1) Every one who
>   **(*a*) being the holder of a judicial office, or being a member of Parliament or of the legislature of a province, corruptly**
>>   **(i) accepts or obtains,**
>>   **(ii) agrees to accept, or**
>>   **(iii) attempts to obtain,**
>>   **any money, valuable consideration, office, place or employment for himself or another person in respect of anything done or omitted or to be done or omitted by him in his official capacity, or**
>   **(*b*) gives or offers, corruptly, to a person mentioned in paragraph (*a*) any money, valuable consideration, office, place or employment in respect of anything done or omitted or to be done or omitted by him in his official capacity for himself or another person,**

is guilty of an indictable offence and liable to imprisonment for a term not exceeding fourteen years.

(2) No proceedings against a person who holds a judicial office shall be instituted under this section without the consent in writing of the Attorney General of Canada. R.S., c. C-34, s. 108.

CROSS-REFERENCES

The term "office" is defined in s. 118. The term "corruptly" is not defined in this Part but has been considered by the courts in relation to the secret commission offence in s. 426 where it was held not to mean wickedly or dishonestly but to refer to an act done *mala fides*, designed wholly or partially for the purpose of bringing about the effect forbidden by the section: *R. v. Brown* (1956), 116 C.C.C. 287 (Ont. C.A.).

This offence may be the basis for an application for an authorization to intercept private communications by reason of s. 183 and falls within the definition of "enterprise crime offence" in s. 462.3 for the purposes of Part XII.2. Conviction for this offence may, in some circumstances, result in loss of the office by virtue of s. 748(1) and other disabilities as prescribed by s. 748(2).

Where the accused is the holder of a judicial office, the consent in writing of the Attorney General of Canada is required (subsec. (2)) and the offence may only be tried by a superior court of criminal jurisdiction (defined in s. 2) by virtue of ss. 468 and 469. [Note, attempt and conspiracy to commit the offence by the holder of a judicial office would not fall within the exclusive jurisdiction of the superior court.] It would also seem that, by virtue of s. 522, only a judge of a superior court can release on bail in such circumstances.

In all other cases, the accused has an election as to mode of trial under s. 536(2) and release pending trial is dealt with under s. 515.

Example 4.2
Related sections and other sources

There is variety and depth of relevant information contained in the Cross-References. It should become a habit to examine the Cross-References applicable to any section for which research is being undertaken, or which is the focus of classroom study and discussion. Whenever the reference is to one of the other statutes contained in *Martin's Criminal Code*, there is the added benefit of having the related statute immediately available. In the case of other relevant legislation, there is a good chance that it will be found in *Martin's Related Criminal Statutes*.

Exercises

4.1 Find the Cross-References under s. 253, Operating While Impaired. Where is "motor vehicle" defined? Where is "operate" defined? Where is the punishment set out?

_____

_____

4.2 Find the Cross-References for s. 175, Causing Disturbance. . . . What are a few of the related offences that an arresting officer should be aware of?

_____

_____

_____

_____

SYNOPSIS

The purpose of the Synopsis is to translate the wording of the section into everyday language. The legalese and structure of a section may be so complicated as to leave one wondering what it actually means. The Synopsis converts the legislative language to wording more easily understood, and it removes the repetitive phrases to provide a basic understanding of what the section seeks to deal with.

Example 4.3

Look at s. 254, Definitions (reproduced on pages 19 to 21). The section is long and complex. However, the Synopsis that follows s. 254 is concise and effectively explains in understandable terms the meaning of the section. It outlines clearly when a breath sample may be taken and when a blood sample may be taken.

In addition to providing a simplified version of a complex section, the Synopsis may include further explanation and analysis.

Note that the Synopsis for s. 265, Assault, indicates that this section applies to all forms of assault, including sexual assault. Consequently, there is no Synopsis following s. 271, Sexual Assault, since this would be repetitive. Instead, the Cross-References under s. 271 refer the reader back to the definition of assault in s. 265.

DEFINITIONS / "analyst" / "approved container" / "approved instrument" / "approved screening device" / "qualified medical practitioner" / "qualified technician" / Testing for presence of alcohol in the blood / Samples of breath or blood where reasonable belief of commission of offence / Exception / Failure or refusal to provide sample / Only one conviction for failure to comply with demand.

254. (1) In this section and sections 255 to 258,

"analyst" means a person designated by the Attorney General as an analyst for the purposes of section 258;

"approved container" means

> *(a)* in respect of breath samples, a container of a kind that is designed to receive a sample of the breath of a person for analysis and is approved as suitable for the purposes of section 258 by order of the Attorney General of Canada, and
>
> *(b)* in respect of blood samples, a container of a kind that is designed to receive a sample of the blood of a person for analysis and is approved as suitable for the purposes of section 258 by order of the Attorney General of Canada;

REGULATIONS: APPROVED BLOOD SAMPLE CONTAINER ORDER
Approved Container

2. The container, Vacutainer ® XF947, being a container of a kind that is designed to receive a sample of the blood of a person for analysis, is hereby approved as suitable, in respect of blood samples, for the purposes of section 258 of the *Criminal Code*. SI/85-199, *Can. Gaz. Part II*, 27/11/85, p. 4690.

"approved instrument" means an instrument of a kind that is designed to receive and make an analysis of a sample of the breath of a person in order to measure the concentration of alcohol in the blood of that person and is approved as suitable for the purposes of section 258 by order of the Attorney General of Canada;

REGULATIONS: APPROVED BREATH ANALYSIS INSTRUMENTS ORDER
Approved Instruments

2. The following instruments, each being an instrument of a kind that is designed to receive and make an analysis of a sample of the breath of a person in order to measure the concentration of alcohol in the blood of that person, are hereby approved as suitable for the purposes of section 258 of the *Criminal Code*:

> *(a)* Breathalyzer®, Model 800;
> *(b)* Breathalyzer®, Model 900;
> *(c)* Breathalyzer®, Model 900A;
> *(d)* Intoximeter Mark IV;
> *(e)* Alcolmeter AE-D1;
> *(f)* Intoxilyzer 4011AS;
> *(g)* Alcotest® 7110;
> *(h)* Intoxilyzer® 5000C;
> *(i)* Breathalyzer®, Model 900B;
> *(j)* Intoxilyzer 1400;
> *(k)* BAC Datamaster C;
> *(l)* Alco-Sensor IV-RBT IV; and
> *(m)* Breathalyzer® 7410-CDN with printer.

SI/85-201, *Can. Gaz. Part II*, 27/11/85, p. 4692; SI/92-105, *Can. Gaz. Part II*, 17/6/92, p. 2577; SI/92-167, *Can. Gaz. Part II*, 23/9/92, p. 3807; SI/93-61, *Can. Gaz., Part II*, 5/5/93, p. 2198; SI/93-175, *Can. Gaz., Part II*, 8/9/93, p. 3714; SOR/94-422, *Can. Gaz., Part II*, 15/6/94, p. 2451; SOR/94-572, *Can. Gaz., Part II*, 7/9/94, p. 3132; SOR/95-312, *Can. Gaz., Part II*, 12/7/95, p. 1885; SOR/2000-200, *Can. Gaz., Part II*, s. 1.

"approved screening device" means a device of a kind that is designed to ascertain the presence of alcohol in the blood of a person and that is approved for the purposes of this section by order of the Attorney General of Canada;

**Example 4.3
A long and complex section of the Code**

REGULATIONS: APPROVED SCREENING DEVICES ORDER
Approved Screening Devices

2. The following devices, each being a device of a kind that is designed to ascertain the presence of alcohol in the blood of a person, are hereby approved for the purposes of section 254 of the *Criminal Code*:

    (a)   Alcolmeter S-L2; and

    (b)   Alco-Sûr;

    (c)   Alcotest® 7410 PA3;

    (d)   Alcotest® 7410 GLC;

    (e)   Alco-Sensor IV DWF;

    (f)   Alco-Sensor IV PWF; and

    (g)   Intoxilyzer 400D.

SI/85-200, *Can. Gaz. Part II,* 27/11/85, p. 4691; **SI/88-136,** *Can. Gaz. Part II,* 28/9/88, p. 4074; **SOR/93-263,** *Can. Gaz., Part II,* 2/6/93, p. 2403; **SOR/94-193,** *Can. Gaz., Part II,* 9/3/94, p. 1232; **SOR/94-423,** *Can. Gaz., Part II,* 15/6/94, p. 2453; **SOR/96-81,** *Can. Gaz., Part II,* 24/1/96, p. 609; **SOR/97-116,** *Can. Gaz., Part II,* 53/97, p. 649.

"qualified medical practitioner" means a person duly qualified by provincial law to practise medicine;

"qualified technician" means,

    (a) in respect of breath samples, a person designated by the Attorney General as being qualified to operate an approved instrument, and

    (b) in respect of blood samples, any person or person of a class of persons designated by the Attorney General as being qualified to take samples of blood for the purposes of this section and sections 256 and 258.

(2) Where a peace officer reasonably suspects that a person who is operating a motor vehicle or vessel or operating or assisting in the operation of an aircraft or of railway equipment or who has the care or control of a motor vehicle, vessel or aircraft or of railway equipment, whether it is in motion or not, has alcohol in the person's body, the peace officer may, by demand made to that person, require the person to provide forthwith such a sample of breath as in the opinion of the peace officer is necessary to enable a proper analysis of the breath to be made by means of an approved screening device and, where necessary, to accompany the peace officer for the purpose of enabling such a sample of breath to be taken.

Note: Subsection (3) does not conform to the R.S.C. 1985 convention which converts the former reference in the phrase "on reasonable and probable grounds" to "on reasonable grounds".

(3) Where a peace officer believes on reasonable and probable grounds that a person is committing, or at any time within the preceding three hours has committed, as a result of the consumption of alcohol, an offence under section 253, the peace officer may, by demand made to that person forthwith or as soon as practicable, require that person to provide then or as soon thereafter as is practicable

    (*a*) such samples of the person's breath as in the opinion of a qualified technician, or

    (*b*) where the peace officer has reasonable and probable grounds to believe that, by reason of any physical condition of the person,

        (i) the person may be incapable of providing a sample of his breath, or

        (ii) it would be impracticable to obtain a sample of his breath,

        such samples of the person's blood, under the conditions referred to in subsection (4), as in the opinion of the qualified medical practitioner or qualified technician taking the samples

are necessary to enable proper analysis to be made in order to determine the concentration, if any, of alcohol in the person's blood, and to accompany the peace officer for the purpose of enabling such samples to be taken.

(4) Samples of blood may only be taken from a person pursuant to a demand made by a peace officer under subsection (3) if the samples are taken by or under the direction of a qualified medical practitioner and the qualified medical practitioner is satisfied that the taking of those samples would not endanger the life or health of the person.

(5) Every one commits an offence who, without reasonable excuse, fails or refuses to comply with a demand made to him by a peace officer under this section.

(6) A person who is convicted of an offence committed under subsection (5) for a failure or refusal to comply with a demand made under subsection (2) or paragraph (3)(*a*) or (*b*) in respect of any transaction may not be convicted of another offence committed under subsection (5) in respect of the same transaction. R.S.C. 1985, c. 27 (1st Supp.), s. 36; c. 1 (4th Supp.), s. 14; c. 32 (4th Supp.), s. 60; 1999, c. 32, s. 2.

CROSS-REFERENCES

The terms "peace officer", "motor vehicle" and "railway equipment" are defined in s. 2. The terms "aircraft", "vessel" and "operates" are defined in s. 214. The procedure for obtaining a warrant to obtain blood samples is set out in s. 256. The adverse inference respecting the impaired offence for failing to comply with a demand under this section is found in s. 258(3). The presumptions respecting the accused's blood alcohol level arising from analysis of a breath sample or blood sample are found in s. 258(1)(*c*), (*d*) and (*d*.1). Procedure for admission of certificates of an analyst, qualified technician and medical practitioner is set out in s. 258(1)(*e*) to (*i*) and (6) and (7). Note s. 258(4) which provides for summary application to a judge within 3 months of the date the blood sample was taken for an order releasing one of the samples for the purpose of testing by the defence.

The punishment for this offence is set out in s. 255. Where the prosecution elects to proceed by indictment on this offence then the accused may elect his mode of trial pursuant to s. 536(2). Where the prosecution elects to proceed by way of summary conviction then the trial of this offence is conducted by a summary conviction court pursuant to Part XXVII. In either case, release pending trial is determined by s. 515, although the accused is eligible for release by a peace officer under s. 496, 497 or by the officer in charge under s. 498. An accused found guilty of this offence is subject to an order prohibiting him from operating a motor vehicle, vessel, aircraft or railway equipment, as the case may be, where the accused was operating or had the care or control of a motor vehicle, vessel, aircraft or railway equipment or was assisting in the operation of an aircraft or of railway equipment at the time the offence was committed or within the two hours preceding that time. The length of the order is as follows: for a first offence, during a period of not more than three years and not less than three months; for a second offence, during a period of not more than three years and not less than six months; for each subsequent offence, during a period of not more than three years and not less than one year. The procedure respecting the making of that order of prohibition is found in s. 260. Pursuant to s. 255.1, evidence that the accused's blood alcohol level exceeded .160 at the time when the offence was committed is deemed to be an aggravating factor on sentencing. Note s. 732.1(3)(*g*.1) and (*g*.2), which allow for imposition of terms of probation that the offender attend for curative treatment in relation to the consumption of alcohol and drugs and participate in an alcohol ignition interlock device program.

Related offences: s. 249, dangerous operation; s. 252, failing to stop at scene of accident; ss. 253 and 255, impaired operation and "over 80"; ss. 220 and 221, criminal negligence causing death or bodily harm.

Section 257 protects the medical practitioner and qualified technician from criminal and civil liability when proceeding under this section.

SYNOPSIS

Subsection (1) defines certain terms relating to breath and blood demands. Subsection (2) states that a peace officer may make a demand for a breath sample from a person who is operating a motor vehicle, vessel, aircraft or railway equipment and whom he *reasonably suspects* has ingested alcohol [the approved screening device or "ALERT" demand]. Under subsec. (3), if the peace officer has *reasonable and probable grounds* to believe that a person is or has, during the preceding three hours, committed an offence under s. 253, the peace officer may make a demand of that person for breath samples [the breathalyzer demand]. When the peace officer has *reasonable and probable grounds* to believe that the physical condition of the person is such that he may not be capable of providing the breath sample or that it would be impractical to do so, a demand may be made that *blood samples* be taken by or under the supervision of a qualified physician as long as the physician is satisfied that this procedure would not endanger the life of the person [blood demand]. It is an offence to refuse to comply with a peace officer's demand under this section, pursuant to subsec. (5). Pursuant to subsec. (6), an accused can only be convicted of an offence under this section arising out of the same transaction.

Example 4.3
A concise explanation of the section

4.3 Read s. 179, Vagrancy / Punishment, carefully and then try to write your own Synopsis. Compare it with the Synopsis provided in Martin's. Did you interpret the wording in a similar way? After reading the Martin's Synopsis, is your understanding of the section improved? Would it have been easier to understand the section if you had read the Martin's Synopsis first?

4.4 Choose and read any section of the *Criminal Code*. Then read the Synopsis and the Cross-References. Was it beneficial to have read the Synopsis before the Cross-References? Choose and read another section, and then read the Cross-References before the Synopsis. Is there a particular order that works better for you?

ANNOTATIONS

Introduction

Annotations are summaries of court decisions (judgments) that focus on how the court interpreted a particular section of a statute, such as the *Criminal Code*. Court decisions that interpret or apply a particular section, or a word or phrase within a section, of the *Criminal Code* have been researched by the authors and editors of Martin's. The relevant and important comments of the court are quoted or explained in the Annotations.

Annotations are a valuable tool. They may be used as a starting point for further research, such as reading the full text of a case, or for finding additional cases. You may find that the Martin's Annotations preclude the need for additional research where a basic understanding of the law is all that is required.

Example 4.4

Look at s. 177, Trespassing at Night. What is meant by "prowls at night"? The Cross-References indicate that "night" is defined in s. 2, but what about "prowls"? Look at the Annotations (reproduced on page 23).

In *R. v. Cloutier* (1991), 66 C.C.C. (3d) 149, the Quebec Court of Appeal held that "[p]rowling involves some notion of evil" and that a prowler has a purpose. A British Columbia lower court in *R. v. Willis* (1987), 37 C.C.C. (3d) 184 (B.C. Co. Ct.) interpreted "prowl" as "to traverse stealthily in the sense of furtively, secretly, clandestinely. . . ."

Definitions stated by provincial courts of appeal and the Supreme Court of Canada are binding on lower courts. This principle of *stare decisis* is explained next.

TRESPASSING AT NIGHT.

177. Every one who, without lawful excuse, the proof of which lies on him, loiters or prowls at night on the property of another person near a dwelling-house situated on that property is guilty of an offence punishable on summary conviction. R.S., c. C-34, s. 173.

CROSS-REFERENCES

The terms "dwelling-house" and "night" are defined in s. 2. While the term "property" is also defined in s. 2, the very broad definition in that provision appears unsuited to the context of this offence. Under s. 494(2), a property owner or person in lawful possession of property and anyone authorized by such person may arrest, without warrant, a person whom he finds committing a criminal offence on or in relation to that property. Reference should also be made to ss. 40 to 42 relating to use of force in defence of dwelling-house and other real property.

The trial of this offence is conducted by a summary conviction court pursuant to Part XXVII. The punishment for the offence is then as set out in s. 787 and the limitation period is set out in s. 786(2). Release pending trial is determined by s. 515, although the accused is eligible for release by a peace officer under s. 496, 497 or by the officer in charge under s. 498.

**Example 4.4
Definition of "night"**

SYNOPSIS

This section makes it a summary conviction offence to *loiter* or *prowl by night* near a dwelling house on another person's property. The accused may raise a lawful excuse but the burden of proving it is upon the accused. As with all sections which place a burden upon the accused, this aspect of the section is likely to attract scrutiny under the *Canadian Charter of Rights and Freedoms*.

ANNOTATIONS

This section creates two offences of prowling and loitering. The essence of loitering is the conduct of someone who is wandering about apparently without precise destination and is conduct which essentially has nothing reprehensible about it, if it does not take place on private property where the loiterer has no business. Prowling, on the other hand, involves some notion of evil. The prowler does not act without a purpose: *R. v. Cloutier* (1991), 66 C.C.C. (3d) 149 (Que. C.A.). Also see: *R. v. McLean* (1970), 1 C.C.C. (2d) 277, 75 W.W.R. 157 (Alta. Mag. Ct.).

Meaning of "prowls"

"Prowls" means to traverse stealthily in the sense of furtively, secretly, clandestinely or moving by imperceptible degrees. The Crown need not prove that the accused was looking for an opportunity to carry out an unlawful purpose. It is not a lawful excuse within the meaning of this section that the accused was trying to conceal himself following commission of a criminal offence: *R. v. Willis* (1987), 37 C.C.C. (3d) 184 (B.C. Co. Ct.).

This section does not create an unconstitutional reverse onus provision inconsistent with the guarantee to the presumption of innocence in s. 11(*d*) of the *Canadian Charter of Rights and Freedoms*: *R. v. Tassou* (1984), 16 C.C.C. (3d) 567 (Alta. Prov. Ct.).

Exercises

4.5 Is there likely to be a conviction under s. 175, Causing Disturbance . . . , where an accused gets into a loud swearing match with a friend in a secluded laneway? How about if there are passersby?

_____

_____

_____

_____

_____

_____

4.6 Paragraph (*d*) of s. 343, Robbery, provides that one commits robbery who "steals . . . while armed with an offensive weapon or imitation thereof". Where the accused holds up his hand with his first finger pointing forward and thumb up, imitating a gun, could he be convicted under para. 343(*d*)?

_____

_____

_____

_____

The Concept of *Stare Decisis* (Precedent Value)

Case law is important for its "precedent" value. *Stare decisis* is the legal principle that dictates that lower courts must follow the rulings of higher courts. Judgments of higher courts set precedents that must be followed by lower courts in their jurisdiction when they hear similar cases. The intention behind this principle is to promote consistency and predictability in the law.

The court structure in Canada is based primarily on geographical location and court level. Each province has its own hierarchy of courts, with authority only within that province. For example, the British Columbia Provincial Court must follow the rulings of the British Columbia Court of Appeal.

There are also several federal courts with jurisdiction throughout the entire country — such as the Supreme Court of Canada, the Federal Court and the Federal Court of Appeal. The Supreme Court of Canada is the ultimate court of appeal for all Canadian courts and is the court of highest jurisdiction in Canada. All Canadian courts must follow the precedents set by the Supreme Court of Canada.

Lower courts do not have to follow rulings made by the courts of other provinces, even the courts of appeal. However, case law from those courts, especially the courts of appeal, may be persuasive (not binding).

Therefore, it is important to take note of the level of court when you are reading annotations, so that you can accurately assess the degree of influence of the judgment. By understanding how courts, particularly higher courts, have interpreted and applied sections of the *Criminal Code* in the past, you will be able to make educated assumptions about how the courts will decide future cases.

 Exercises

4.7 Subparagraph 1(*a*)(iii) of s. 175, Causing Disturbance . . . , provides that everyone who causes a disturbance in or near a public place (not in a dwelling-house), by "impeding or molesting" others, has committed the offence. Has it become

easier or more difficult to convict on this charge since 1980?
(Hint: look at the Annotations for para. 175(1)(*a*).)

_____

_____

_____

_____

_____

_____

_____

4.8 The Quebec case of *R. v. Gouchie* (1976), 33 C.C.C. (2d) 120 (Que. Sess. Peace), referenced in the Annotations for s. 343, Robbery, was decided by a lower court. Is there another case that might be more persuasive in arguing that a hand gesture does not constitute an imitation of an offensive weapon?

_____

_____

_____

_____

_____

_____

_____

_____

_____

Disagreement Among Courts

Despite the principle of *stare decisis*, courts often make decisions that conflict with the decisions of other courts. Sometimes this is because the point of law at issue has not yet been heard by a higher court, so that lower courts are not bound by precedent. Often contradictory judgments exist among courts of the same level, but in different jurisdictions. The law may therefore differ in different provinces, even with respect to the *Criminal Code*, until a case on point is appealed to the Supreme Court of Canada and a definitive ruling of national scope is made.

Contradictory cases are flagged in the Annotations by the word *contra* preceding a citation. ***Contra*** indicates that there is disagreement about a point of law. Such a case may still be persuasive if the court's analysis of the facts and law is applicable to the facts and law relating to the file for which you are doing research. However, remember that when you are doing legal research, it is important to examine all sides of the argument, including cases that go against your position.

Example 4.5

Look at the Annotations for s. 258, Proceedings Under Section 255, following the heading "Right to production of ampoules, etc." The seventh paragraph after that heading (reproduced on page 27) begins, "Failure of the prosecution to supply the accused with a sample of the alcohol standard does not violate s. 7 of the Charter". The case citation immediately following indicates that this conclusion was reached by the court in *R. v. Gascon* (1987), 50 M.V.R. 213 (Ont. Prov. Ct.). Immediately following the *Gascon* citation is *Contra: R. v. Kalafut* (1988), 70 Sask. R. 94(Q.B.). This reference indicates that the judgment of the Saskatchewan Queen's Bench in *Kalafut* contradicts the *Gascon* judgment and holds that the failure to provide the standard does in fact violate s. 7 of the Charter.

Two paragraphs below, there is an example of a disagreement between the Nova Scotia Court of Appeal and the Alberta Court of Appeal. The contentious issue is whether s. 7 and para. 11(*d*) of the Charter are infringed by a refusal to allow the person engaged in breath sample testing to view the testing instrument's gauge.

The Nova Scotia Court of Appeal in *R. v. Selig* (1991), 4 C.R. (4th) 20 held that the Charter sections were infringed in such circumstances. The Alberta Court of Appeal disagreed and held that they were not in *R. v. Gillis* (1994), 91 C.C.C. (3d) 575.

Ratio Decidendi and *Obiter Dicta*

The terms *ratio decidendi* and *obiter dicta* refer to two types of statements made by the court. The **ratio decidendi** is the specific ruling or legal principle declared. It is often referred to simply as the "*ratio*", and it is binding on lower courts.

Obiter dicta (or, in the singular, **obiter dictum**) consist of opinions stated by the court that do not directly affect the outcome of the decision. These opinions (often referred to simply as "*obiter*") are generally not binding on lower courts. The exception is *obiter* within judgments of the Supreme Court of Canada, which are binding on other courts. (In *R. v. Sellars*, [1980] 1 S.C.R. 527, the Supreme Court stated that where it rules on a point, any declaration made in the ruling, even though not absolutely necessary to dispose of the appeal, must be followed and applied by all lower courts.)

Case Name (Style of Cause)

The case name is also called the "style of cause". In Canada, the case name used for criminal cases is generally "*R. v. [the last name of the accused]*". Case names are italicized when referenced in law books and reports.

Because Canada is a constitutional monarchy, prosecutors of criminal cases represent the reigning monarch — currently Queen Elizabeth. The concept of

Right to production of ampoules, etc. – In *R. v. Duke*, [1972] S.C.R. 917, 7 C.C.C. (2d) 474, 18 C.R.N.S. 302, it was held (9:0) that because Parliament specifically proclaimed the predecessor to this section in force, in the manner that it did, the failure of the Crown to provide the suspected driver with a sample of his breath did not deprive him of his right to a fair hearing.

Similarly, the routine non-malicious destruction of the ampoules so that the accused is unable to conduct his own tests of the ampoules does not deprive the accused of a fair hearing or of his rights under the Charter: *R. v. Potma* (1983), 2 C.C.C. (3d) 383, 31 C.R. (3d) 231, 144 D.L.R. (3d) 620 (Ont. C.A.), leave to appeal to S.C.C. refused D.L.R. *loc. cit.*

Section 7 of the Charter requires the Crown to make disclosure and discovery of relevant materials and in this case this included providing representative samples of the ampoules from the same lot as those used to test the accused so that independent tests could be conducted to ascertain the reliability and accuracy of the machine when such ampoules are used. In this case the ampoules were not those recommended for use by the machine's manufacturer: *R. v. Bourget* (1987), 35 C.C.C. (3d) 371, 56 C.R. (3d) 97, 46 M.V.R. 246 (Sask. C.A.).

However, it was held in *R. v. Eagles* (1989), 47 C.C.C. (3d) 129, 68 C.R. (3d) 271, 88 N.S.R. (2d) 337 (C.A.), that the accused was not entitled to a sample of the ampoule in the absence of some factual foundation or other basis shown indicating that production and examination of the representative ampoule would advance the defence. And, a similar test was applied in *R. v. Delaney* (1989), 48 C.C.C. (3d) 276, 13 M.V.R. (2d) 1 (N.S.C.A.), where an application was made by the accused for an order permitting access by a defence expert to the breathalyzer machine upon which the accused had been tested. It was held that the application should have been dismissed, the first request for inspection not having been made in a timely fashion and it not being shown in what way mere inspection of the machine might assist the accused's case.

Similarly, in *R. v. Lefebvre* (1988), 90 A.R. 334, 9 M.V.R. (2d) 304 (Q.B.), it was held that failure to furnish representative samples of the ampoules was not a violation of s. 7. In this case, the evidence indicated that the warning referred to in *R. v. Bourget, supra*, had been withdrawn by the manufacturer. Further, evidence accepted by the trial judge indicated that it was highly unlikely that a random sample of the ampoule would be found to be faulty and even if it were it could not affect the tests administered by the technician. The standard alcohol test would demonstrate the accuracy of the breathalyzer. Finally, the ampoule actually used in the test of the accused is of no value.

It was held in *R. v. Hodgson* (1990), 57 C.C.C. (3d) 278, 78 C.R. (3d) 333, 24 M.V.R. (2d) 42 (B.C.C.A.), that there was no reasonable basis for concluding that the failure to preserve a representative sample of the alcohol standard infringed the accused's rights to make full answer and defence and to be tried in accordance with the principles of fundamental justice as guaranteed by s. 7 of the Charter. Counsel could only speculate that independent analysis of the sample could have disclosed that it was not suitable for use in the breathalyzer and there were other means to determine the issue, for example, by obtaining the chemical composition from the analyst who prepared it or by resorting to the opinion of an expert. Further, the Crown had acted fairly by informing defence counsel of the name of the analyst and offering to provide a sample if the particular lot had not been exhausted.

Failure of the prosecution to supply the accused with a sample of the alcohol standard does not violate s. 7 of the Charter: *R. v. Gascon* (1987), 50 M.V.R. 213 (Ont. Prov. Ct.). *Contra: R. v. Kalafut* (1988), 70 Sask. R. 94, 8 M.V.R. (2d) 185 (Q.B.).

Failure of the officer to show the accused the reading on the breathalyzer did not deprive the accused of a fair trial. The officer had been willing to do so but, by the time the request was made, the reading had been erased: *R. v. Cabanela* (1989), 25 M.V.R. (2d) 161 (Ont. C.A.).

The accused's rights under ss. 7 and 11(*d*) of the Charter were infringed when his polite request to view the breathalyzer gauge at the time the tests were being administered was refused. Viewing the readings would have assisted the accused in making full answer and defence and would not have interfered in the administration of the tests: *R. v. Selig* (1991), 4 C.R. (4th) 20, 27 M.V.R. (2d) 166, 101 N.S.R. (2d) 281 (C.A.). *Contra: R. v. Gillis* (1994), 91 C.C.C. (3d) 575, 63 W.A.C. 395, 149 A.R. 395 (C.A.).

Also see Lucas, D.M. "Production of Breathalyzer Material", (1989), 1 J.M.V.L. 103.

On this issue, also see the note by C. Finley, "Production Requests: The Crown's Duty to Provide", 21 M.V.R. (2d) 65.

**Example 4.5
Contradictory
judgments**

the monarch as prosecutor reflects centuries of development of the criminal law in England. Historically, all offences stemmed from a breach of the monarch's peace and protection sheltering every citizen of the realm. (In contrast, in the United States, which is a republic, the prosecutor is the representative of "The People".)

This is why prosecutions are cited as *R. v. [the last name of the accused]*. *R.* stands for either *Rex* (King) or *Regina* (Queen); *v.* is the abbreviation of *versus*, the Latin word meaning "against". Thus, *R. v. Abbott* is read as *Regina* (or *Rex* if the ruling monarch is a male) *versus Abbott*.

Initialized Case Names

Where there is a prohibition against publication of the name of the accused, the case name uses initials. This applies to cases involving youth, because disclosure of the accused's identity is prohibited under the *Youth Criminal Justice Act* (and its predecessor, the *Young Offenders Act*).

Alternatively, there may be a court order prohibiting publication of the name of an adult accused in certain cases. For example, if publication of the name of the accused will likely reveal the identity of a complainant in a sexual offence case, the court will order non-publication of the accused's name as well as the complainant's name.

Such a case is *R. v. A.(A.)* (2001), 155 C.C.C. (3d) 279 (Ont. C.A.), which can be found under the Annotations for s. 273.1. At the accused's first trial, an order was made banning the publication of the name of the complainant, but not the name of the accused. When the Court of Appeal ordered a new trial for the accused, it not only banned publication of the identity of the complainant, but also prohibited publication of the identity of the accused. The reason was that publication of the accused's name would likely reveal the identity of the complainant.

A publication prohibition continues until a court orders otherwise. A violation of a non-publication order created by legislation such as the *Youth Criminal Justice Act* or s. 486 of the *Criminal Code*, or by a judge's common law powers, may be prosecuted as an offence under the relevant statute or by contempt proceedings.

Understanding Legal Citations

The case name (style of cause) is followed by a citation, which provides information about the case and how to locate the full-text judgment. There may be multiple citations for any particular case, since many cases are reported (published) in more than one law report. This provides choice for a researcher who wants to look up a case. Note, however, that not all citations will necessarily be listed. The following is a list of reports you may encounter:

ABBREVIATION	TITLE
Canadian reports	
Alta. L.R.	Alberta Law Reports
A.R.	Alberta Reports
B.C.L.R.	British Columbia Law Reports
C.C.C.	Canadian Criminal Cases
C.R.	Criminal Reports
C.R.N.S.	Criminal Reports New Series
D.L.R.	Dominion Law Reports
Man. R.	Manitoba Reports
M.V.R.	Motor Vehicle Reports
N.B.R.	New Brunswick Reports
Nfld. & P.E.I.R.	Newfoundland and Prince Edward Island Reports
N.R.	National Reporter
N.S.R.	Nova Scotia Reports
O.A.C.	Ontario Appeal Cases
O.L.R.	Ontario Law Reports
O.R.	Ontario Reports
Sask. R.	Saskatchewan Reports
S.C.R.	Supreme Court Reports
W.A.C.	Western Appeal Cases
W.C.B.	Weekly Criminal Bulletin
W.W.R.	Western Weekly Reports

English criminal law reports

Cr. App. R.	Criminal Appeal Reports

Example 4.6

Look at *R. v. Mid Valley Tractor Sales Ltd.* (1995), 101 C.C.C. (3d) 253, 167 N.B.R. (2d) 161 (C.A.), in the Annotations for s. 632, Excusing Jurors (reproduced on page 30).

For this case, citations are provided for the Canadian Criminal Cases (C.C.C.) and the New Brunswick Reports (N.B.R.). The number preceding the report name — for example, "167" preceding "N.B.R." — refers to the volume number of the report. The notation "(2d)" following "N.B.R." refers to "second series". The number "161" following "(2d)"

ANNOTATIONS

The pre-screening procedure in which the trial judge directs questions to the jury panel to deal with cases of obvious partiality, as where the juror is related to the accused or a witness, is part of the trial and must be done in the presence of the accused: *R. v. Barrow*, [1987] 2 S.C.R. 694, 38 C.C.C. (3d) 193, 61 C.R. (3d) 305 (5:2).

As this initial procedure goes only to such clear-cut cases of partiality, the consent of counsel is and can be presumed. Once out of obvious situations of non-indifference, the consent can no longer be presumed and the procedure must conform to that set out in the *Criminal Code*, including the procedure for challenge for cause. The trial judge has no right to take over the challenge process by deciding controversial questions of partiality. If there exist legitimate grounds for a challenge for cause, outside of the obvious cases, it must proceed in accordance with the Code: *R. v. Sherratt*, [1991] 1 S.C.R. 509, 63 C.C.C. (3d) 193, 3 C.R. (4th) 129 (5:0), approving *R. v. Guérin and Pimparé* (1984), 13 C.C.C. (3d) 231 (Que. C.A.). See also *R. v. Betker* (1997), 115 C.C.C. (3d) 421, 7 C.R. (5th) 238, *sub nom. R. v. B. (A.)* (Ont. C.A.), leave to appeal to S.C.C. refused 121 C.C.C. (3d) vi, noted under s. 638.

This provision does not allow the judge to delegate the power to excuse jurors. Furthermore, potential jurors should not be excused in private as the accused and the public must be able to know the reasons for any decision to excuse. Consequently, the trial judge erred when he asked the sheriff to pre-screen additional jurors in the absence of the accused when the jury panel had been exhausted: *R. v. Mid Valley Tractor Sales Ltd.* (1995), 101 C.C.C. (3d) 253, 167 N.B.R. (2d) 161 (C.A.).

The trial judge was entitled to dismiss the juror where the triers of cause were unable to agree on a challenge for cause in respect of a prospective juror: *R. v. Gayle* (2001), 154 C.C.C. (3d) 221, 201 D.L.R. (4th) 540 (Ont. C.A.), leave to appeal to S.C.C. refused 159 C.C.C. (3d) vi, 207 D.L.R. (4th) vi.

The inquiry into hardship must occur prior to the challenge for cause process and exercise of peremptory challenges: *R. v. Douglas* (2002), 170 C.C.C. (3d) 126, 12 C.R. (6th) 374, 62 O.R. (3d) 583 (C.A.).

Example 4.6
Reading case citations

refers to the number of the page on which the case report begins. In other words, this case can be found on page 161 of volume 167 of the second series of the New Brunswick Reports.

At the end of the citation is "(C.A.)", which indicates the court level — in this case, the Court of Appeal. Because only New Brunswick cases are reported in the N.B.R., it can be concluded that this refers to the New Brunswick Court of Appeal.

Immediately following the case name is the year in which the judgment was reported. The year the judgment was reported often corresponds to the year the judgment was given, but not always.

The year in the above example, 1995, is shown with parentheses (round brackets). This format is used for citations to law reports that do not require you to know the year in order to look up the judgment. For both the C.C.C. and the N.B.R., the volume number alone tells you where you can find the case report.

Example 4.7

Some law reports, such as the Supreme Court Reports (S.C.R.), do require you to know the year in order to look up the case. The year is printed on each volume of the reports. For these citations, the year is shown in square brackets. An example is *R. v. Barrow*, the first case cited in the Annotations for s. 632 (reproduced below). The notation "[1987] 2" tells you that the judgment can be found in the second volume of the reports of cases decided by the Supreme Court in 1987.

ANNOTATIONS

The pre-screening procedure in which the trial judge directs questions to the jury panel to deal with cases of obvious partiality, as where the juror is related to the accused or a witness, is part of the trial and must be done in the presence of the accused: *R. v. Barrow*, [1987] 2 S.C.R. 694, 38 C.C.C. (3d) 193, 61 C.R. (3d) 305 (5:2).

As this initial procedure goes only to such clear-cut cases of partiality, the consent of counsel is and can be presumed. Once out of obvious situations of non-indifference, the consent can no longer be presumed and the procedure must conform to that set out in the *Criminal Code*, including the procedure for challenge for cause. The trial judge has no right to take over the challenge process by deciding controversial questions of partiality. If there exist legitimate grounds for a challenge for cause, outside of the obvious cases, it must proceed in accordance with the Code: *R. v. Sherratt*, [1991] 1 S.C.R. 509, 63 C.C.C. (3d) 193, 3 C.R. (4th) 129 (5:0), approving *R. v. Guérin and Pimparé* (1984), 13 C.C.C. (3d) 231 (Que. C.A.). See also *R. v. Betker* (1997), 115 C.C.C. (3d) 421, 7 C.R. (5th) 238, *sub nom. R. v. B. (A.)* (Ont. C.A.), leave to appeal to S.C.C. refused 121 C.C.C. (3d) vi, noted under s. 638.

This provision does not allow the judge to delegate the power to excuse jurors. Furthermore, potential jurors should not be excused in private as the accused and the public must be able to know the reasons for any decision to excuse. Consequently, the trial judge erred when he asked the sheriff to pre-screen additional jurors in the absence of the accused when the jury panel had been exhausted: *R. v. Mid Valley Tractor Sales Ltd.* (1995), 101 C.C.C. (3d) 253, 167 N.B.R. (2d) 161 (C.A.).

The trial judge was entitled to dismiss the juror where the triers of cause were unable to agree on a challenge for cause in respect of a prospective juror: *R. v. Gayle* (2001), 154 C.C.C. (3d) 221, 201 D.L.R. (4th) 540 (Ont. C.A.), leave to appeal to S.C.C. refused 159 C.C.C. (3d) vi, 207 D.L.R. (4th) vi.

The inquiry into hardship must occur prior to the challenge for cause process and exercise of peremptory challenges: *R. v. Douglas* (2002), 170 C.C.C. (3d) 126, 12 C.R. (6th) 374, 62 O.R. (3d) 583 (C.A.).

Example 4.7
Reading case citations

Infra and *Supra*

Text that refers to cases, as in a law book such as Martin's or a research paper, may use the Latin terms *infra* and *supra* in the place of a case citation or other reference. When **infra** is used, it tells you that additional information relevant to the matter being examined is located farther on in the text.

Example 4.8

In the Annotations for s. 258, there is a short paragraph following the heading "Evidence to the contrary / generally" (reproduced below). Look at the reference to the case of *R. v. Proudlock*, which lists the citations and then states "noted under s. 348, *infra*".

Evidence to the contrary / generally – As to the meaning generally of the words "any evidence to the contrary" see *R. v. Proudlock*, [1979] 1 S.C.R. 525, 43 C.C.C. (2d) 321, 5 C.R. (3d) 21, noted under s. 348, *infra*.

Example 4.8
Annotations
for s. 258: *infra*

Now look at the Annotations for s. 348, in the paragraph following the heading "Presumption of intent [subsec. (2)]" (reproduced below). Here you will find further discussion of *R. v. Proudlock*, as referred to in the commentary on s. 258.

**Example 4.8
Annotations
for s. 348**

Presumption of intent [subsec. (2)] – Once a *prima facie* case is made out using this presumption the accused need only raise a reasonable doubt, which he may do by adducing evidence of an explanation that may reasonably be true. However, an explanation that is disbelieved does not constitute "any evidence to the contrary" as it is no evidence. The evidence upon which the accused relies must at least raise a reasonable doubt as to his guilt, and if it does not meet this test then the *prima facie* case remains: *R. v. Proudlock*, [1979] 1 S.C.R. 525, 43 C.C.C. (2d) 321, 5 C.R. (3d) 21. [**Note:** Since this decision the *Criminal Code* has been amended to delete the word "any" from the phrase "in the absence of any evidence to the contrary". However, the majority judgment in *R. v. Proudlock* indicates that there is no basis for a distinction depending on the presence of the word "any"; the phrases "evidence to the contrary" and "any evidence to the contrary" both being the converse of "no evidence to the contrary".]

Supra is the opposite of *infra* and refers the reader to an earlier part of the text. *Supra* often appears immediately following a case name instead of a citation. It indicates that the case has been cited previously and the editors of the text chose not to repeat the full citation.

Example 4.9

In the Annotations for s. 255, Punishment, following the heading "Circumstances where discharge should be granted", find the paragraph beginning "In determining . . ." (reproduced on page 33). There is a reference to *R. v. Soosay* with citations. The next paragraph contains another reference to the same case, but uses *supra* instead of the citations. *Supra* refers you back to the previous paragraph to find the citations.

Pre-Charter Judgments

The *Canadian Charter of Rights and Freedoms* came into force on April 17, 1982. When you are considering the rulings in cases that were decided before that time, some caution is required. While many of the rights and principles of fundamental justice guaranteed by the Charter were recognized in Canadian law before the Charter, these rights and principles achieved constitutional status when the Charter was included in the *Constitution Act, 1982*.

The Supreme Court of Canada was quick to distinguish the Charter from the Canadian Bill of Rights, the primary statute providing for rights before the Charter. Where the Bill of Rights was viewed as merely another Act of Parliament, the Charter, as a constitutional document, was viewed as "purposive". The

Circumstances where discharge should be granted – Where this subsection has been proclaimed in force, the court is entitled to assume that adequate facilities will be provided for curative treatment. Before invoking this subsection the court must be satisfied on a balance of probabilities that the accused is in need of curative treatment and that a discharge would not be contrary to the public interest. However, notwithstanding the accused has a lengthy record for *Criminal Code* driving offences this subsection may be resorted to where evidence adduced shows that the appropriate treatment for the accused's addiction is available and that the accused is now well-motivated and has a good chance of overcoming his alcoholism: *R. v. Beaulieu* (1980), 53 C.C.C. 342, 7 M.V.R. 9 (N.W.T.S.C.).

In considering whether a curative discharge would be contrary to the public interest, the court should consider, among other things, the circumstances of the offence and whether the accused was involved in an accident causing death, bodily harm or significant property damage; the *bona fides* of the accused; the accused's criminal record as it relates to alcohol-related driving offences; whether the accused was subject to a driving prohibition at the time of the offence; whether the accused had received the benefit of a prior curative discharge and what, if anything, the accused had done to facilitate his rehabilitation under the prior discharge: *R. v. Storr* (1995), 102 W.A.C. 65, 174 A.R. 65 (C.A.).

It will not always be contrary to the public interest to grant a discharge under this subsection to a recidivist. In some cases public protection may well be best served by effective measures to reduce the risk of repetition of the offence through rehabilitation of the offender. On the other hand it would be contrary to the public interest to grant a discharge if there was a real risk of repetition of the offence: *R. v. Wallner* (1988), 44 C.C.C. (3d) 358, 66 C.R. (3d) 79 (Alta. C.A.).

It was improper for the trial judge to adjourn the sentencing of the accused for a lengthy period of time presumably to determine whether he was an appropriate candidate for a discharge for curative treatment by seeing whether he would stop drinking. If the evidence was not sufficient at the time of the application for the discharge, then the judge should have invited the accused to call medical or other evidence: *R. v. Kidder* (1992), 127 A.R. 136, 38 M.V.R. (2d) 98 (C.A.).

In determining whether to grant a discharge, regard must be had to the circumstances and gravity of the offence, the motive of the offender to rehabilitate, the alcohol-related criminal record, whether there was a driving prohibition at the time and whether a previous curative discharge had been granted: *R. v. Soosay* (2001), 160 C.C.C. (3d) 437, 293 A.R. 292, 257 W.A.C. 292 (C.A.).

**Example 4.9
First reference**

"Other evidence" must be evidence which is similar in quality and kind to medical evidence including evidence from other professionals who are able to provide information on treatment and rehabilitation. Accordingly, evidence of the accused and a youth justice committee worker was insufficient to support a discharge: *R. v. Soosay, supra.*

**Second
reference:** *supra*

courts, particularly the Supreme Court of Canada, have assumed much more discretion in their interpretation of the rights asserted by the Charter and have interpreted those rights in a much broader fashion. As a consequence, many of the post-Charter judgments have made significant changes to the law.

When reading annotations, it is prudent to be aware of the date of a particular case. Was the case decided before 1982? If so, the court's rulings in the case may no longer be considered "good law". The issue may have since been re-examined in light of the Charter, and the courts' decisions and reasoning may have changed. In other words, the law has changed. Martin's often provides information about such changes in the Annotations.

Although there have been more than 20 years of development of the law since the Charter was enacted, there are still issues that have yet to be re-examined in the context of the Charter. Other issues have been considered by lower courts but not yet heard by the Supreme Court of Canada. With respect to these issues, there is no clear understanding of what the current law is.

Example 4.10

Look at the Annotations for s. 258. In the first paragraph following the heading "Effect of absence of grounds for making demand" (reproduced below), there is a reference to the Supreme Court of Canada's judgment in *R. v. Rilling*, [1976] 2 S.C.R. 183. The Supreme Court held that the absence of reasonable and probable grounds for believing that an offence of impairment or "over 80" had been committed did not make the certificate of a qualified technician inadmissible as evidence.

It is then explained that this judgment must be considered in light of the Charter. Several other cases are annotated, some of which declare *Rilling* to no longer be "good law" and some of which state that it is. The last word on the issue will have to come from the Supreme Court of Canada.

**Example 4.10
Effect of the *Charter
of Rights and
Freedoms***

Effect of absence of grounds for making demand – While absence of reasonable and probable grounds for belief of impairment [or *semble* as result of the recent amendments, belief that the offence under s. 253(*b*) was committed] may afford a defence to a charge under s. 254(5) it does not render inadmissible certificate evidence of a qualified technician on a charge under s. 237: *R. v. Rilling*, [1976] 2 S.C.R. 183, 24 C.C.C. (2d) 81, 31 C.R.N.S. 142 (5:3). [However, consider now the impact of ss. 8 and 24(2) of the *Charter of Rights and Freedoms*.]

The amendment to [now] s. 254 to authorize a demand not only for an alleged breach of the impaired offence but also the "over 80" offence has not changed the effect of *R. v. Rilling*, *supra*, and thus, subject to the possible effect of the *Charter of Rights and Freedoms*, the law remains that the certificate is admissible although the Crown fails to prove that the officer had the requisite reasonable and probable grounds: *R. v. Linttell* (1991), 64 C.C.C. (3d) 507 (Alta. C.A.).

The question of whether or not the decision in *R. v. Rilling, supra*, can still represent the law in light of the Charter, and especially the guarantee to protection against unreasonable search and seizure in s. 8, has been considered by a number of courts. For example, the following courts have held that *Rilling* is no longer the law: *R. v. Bajkov* (1988), 8 M.V.R. (2d) 213 (B.C.S.C.); *R. v. Wilson* (1985), 42 Sask. R. 181, 22 C.R.R. 32, 37 M.V.R. 203 (Q.B.); *R. v. Dennehy* (1986), 26 C.C.C. (3d) 339 (Y. Terr. Ct.), while the following courts have continued to apply *Rilling*; *R. v. Kiskotagan* (1986), 49 Sask. R. 10, 41 M.V.R. 161 (Q.B.); In *R. v. Marshall* (1989), 91 N.S.R. (2d) 211, 13 M.V.R. (2d) 251 (C.A.), the issue was left open because no application had been made at trial pursuant to s. 24 of the Charter. On the other hand, in *R. v. Wason* (1987), 35 C.R.R. 285, 7 M.V.R. (2d) 88 (Ont. C.A.), the court, without referring to *Rilling*, excluded evidence obtained as a result of a breathalyzer demand because the officer had no reasonable and probable grounds for making the demand which had been based on an improper approved screening device demand under s. 254(2).

It was held in *R. v. Dwernychuk* (1992), 77 C.C.C. (3d) 385, 135 A.R. 31, 42 M.V.R. (2d) 237 (C.A.), leave to appeal to S.C.C. refused 79 C.C.C. (3d) vi, 14 C.R.R. (2d) 192*n*, 151 N.R. 400*n*, that until the Supreme Court of Canada reconsiders *R. v. Rilling, supra*, the lower courts are bound by that decision and thus the lack of reasonable and probable grounds does not affect the admissibility of the certificate.

The absence of reasonable and probable grounds to make the demand will not necessarily result in a violation of the guarantee against arbitrary detention under s. 9 of the *Charter of Rights and Freedoms*, so as to require a determination whether the evidence of the certificate should be excluded under s. 24(2) of the Charter: *R. v. Moore* (1988), 45 C.C.C. (3d) 410, 9 M.V.R. (2d) 190 (N.S.C.A.).

5 Criminal Code Concordance

AMENDMENT, REPEAL AND REVISION

Changes to provisions of the *Criminal Code* are frequently made by Parliament, to make the Code more responsive to the realities of our changing society. For example, numerous changes were made in recent years to tighten the provisions against impaired driving. These changes are called "amendments".

Sometimes sections are removed from the Code. This kind of change is called "repeal". Sometimes completely new sections are added to the Code.

Sometimes the changes are so extensive that it becomes necessary to change section numbers and even renumber entire Parts of the Code. This renumbering is called "revision".

The last major revision of the Code occurred with R.S.C. 1985, c. C-46. (This reference tells you that the revised *Criminal Code* was published by the Government of Canada in the Revised Statutes of Canada, 1985, and that it is located in chapter C-46.)

Changes to the section numbers of provisions can present an obstacle for researchers. Court decisions, which interpret and apply particular sections, do not reflect changes to section numbering that occur after the date of the decision. References to section numbers in judgments given before the last *Criminal Code* revision will refer to the old section number(s) of an earlier version of the Code. This can be confusing. The *Criminal Code* Concordance matches up the old and new section numbers for the same provision.

Consider s. 322 of the *Criminal Code*. This section defines the substantive of-fence of theft. Theft is an offence with a long history; therefore, many judgments are referred to in the Annotations following s. 322, some of which pre-date the 1985 revision to the *Criminal Code*. If you look up any of the older judgments, you will find that they refer to s. 283, which was the previous section number for the offence of theft.

If you do not know the previous section number for a particular provision of the current Code, how can you find it? If a section number referred to in a judgment does not match up to the section in Martin's, what do you do?

The *Criminal Code* Concordance provides cross-references for the Part and section numbers used in R.S.C. 1985, c. C-46 and those used in the preceding revision, R.S.C. 1970, c. C-34. These cross-references will give you the missing information. The Concordance is located at the front of the book, immediately following the Preface.

The Concordance consists of two columns of references; the left-hand column lists the previous Part and section numbers in the 1970 revision, and the right-hand column lists the current Part and section numbers for the 1985 revision, as well as subsequent amendments.

Example 5.1

Find current s. 322 (Theft), in the R.S.C. 1985, c. C-46 column, on the right (reproduced below). It is shown as the second provision in Part IX. If you look across to the left-hand column, you will see that the previous number for the section of-fence of theft was s. 283, which was in Part VII of R.S.C. 1970, c. C-34.

Thus, the Concordance tells you that the section for the offence of theft was s. 283 from 1970 to 1985, at which time it was re-numbered s. 322.

The Concordance may also provide additional information about the status of a section, such as information about repeal.

Example 5.1 Renumbering of sections

R.S.C. 1970, c. C-34	R.S.C. 1985, c. C-46
281.3(8)(a.1)	320(8)(b)
281.3(8)(b)	320(8)(c)
281.3(8)(c)	320(8)(d)
—	320.1 [en. 2001, c. 41, s. 10]
Part VII	Part IX
282	321
283	322
284	323
285	324
286	325
287	326
287.1	327
288	328

Example 5.2

Find subsec. 271(2) in the R.S.C. 1985, c. C-46 column, on the right (reproduced below). Look across to the left-hand column, and you will see the corresponding reference to subsec. 246.1(2) in R.S.C. 1970, c. C-34.

As in Example 5.1, the Concordance tells us that when the *Criminal Code* was revised in 1985, subsec. 246.1(2) was renumbered as subsec. 271(2). However, we also find the following additional information: "[rep. R.S.C. 1985, c. 19 (3rd Supp.), s. 10]".

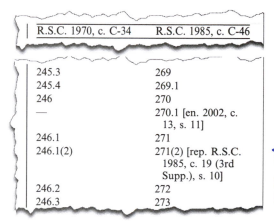

R.S.C. 1970, c. C-34	R.S.C. 1985, c. C-46
245.3	269
245.4	269.1
246	270
—	270.1 [en. 2002, c. 13, s. 11]
246.1	271
246.1(2)	271(2) [rep. R.S.C. 1985, c. 19 (3rd Supp.), s. 10]
246.2	272
246.3	273

Example 5.2
Repealed provision

This means that subsec. 271(2) was repealed by s. 10, found in the Revised Statutes of Canada, 1985, chapter 19, third supplement. Since it was repealed, this subsection is no longer in force, and it is not included in the current version of the *Criminal Code*. (If you look for this subsection in Martin's *Criminal Code*, you will see that it is not reproduced, but the information about its repeal is provided.)

Sometimes only the word "repealed" is found in the right-hand column of the Concordance. This means that the section was removed from the Code, not renumbered, and therefore it is no longer in force.

Example 5.3

For example, find s. 13 in the R.S.C. 1970, c. C-34 column (reproduced to the right). The Concordance indicates that previous s. 13 was repealed by R.S.C. 1985, c. C-46. Because it no longer applies, that provision is not included in the current version of the *Criminal Code*. There is a s. 13 in the current Code, but it is a different provision.

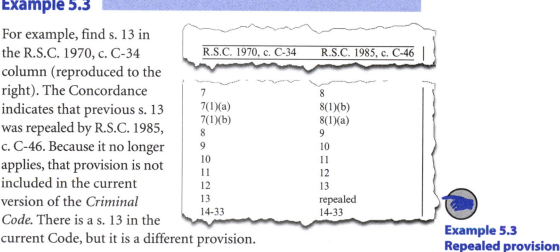

R.S.C. 1970, c. C-34	R.S.C. 1985, c. C-46
7	8
7(1)(a)	8(1)(b)
7(1)(b)	8(1)(a)
8	9
9	10
10	11
11	12
12	13
13	repealed
14-33	14-33

Example 5.3
Repealed provision

The revision of 1985 and further amendments after that date created entirely new Parts to the *Criminal Code* and renumbered other Parts.

Example 5.4

An example of a new Part can be found on the page of the Concordance reproduced to the left. In the R.S.C. 1985, c. C-46 column, look at the entry "Part XXI.1 [en. 2002, c. 13, s. 71]". This means that an entirely new Part (Part XXI.1) was enacted in an amendment in 2002, numbered as s. 71 in chapter 13 of that amending Act.

**Example 5.4
Enactment of
a new Part**

R.S.C. 1970, c. C-34	R.S.C. 1985, c. C-46
624	696
—	Part XXI.1 [en. 2002, c. 13, s. 71]
625	697
626	698
627	699

Example 5.5

An example of renumbering of Parts can be found on the next page of the Concordance, reproduced to the left. Part XXII in R.S.C. 1970, c. C-34 became Part XXV in R.S.C. 1985, c. C-46; Part XXIII became Part XXVI; and Part XXIV became Part XXVII.

**Example 5.5
Renumbering of
Parts**

R.S.C. 1970, c. C-34	R.S.C. 1985, c. C-46
695	760
695.1	761
Part XXII	Part XXV
696	762
697	763
698	764
699	765
700	766
701	767
701.1	767.1
702	768
703	769
704	770
705	771
706	772
707	773
Part XXIII	Part XXVI
708	774
—	774.1 [en. 2002, c. 13, s. 77]
709	775
710	776
711	777
712	778
713	779
714	780
715	781
716	782
717	783
718	repealed
719	784
Part XXIV	Part XXVII
720	785
—	785 "sentence" (*d*) [en. 1997, c. 19, s. 76]

Exercises

5.1 Look up the current s. 487, Information for Search Warrant, in the Concordance. What was the number of this section before the 1985 Revised Statutes of Canada were published?

_____

5.2 Did para. 487(1)(c.1), which allows for the search of "any offence-related property", exist in 1985 when the last Revised Statutes of Canada were published?

_____

_____

_____

_____

HISTORICAL OFFENCES: "COLD CASES"

The Concordance is useful when you are dealing with a historical offence or "cold case". These are cases that involve conduct that occurred years in the past, and often the section numbers of the *Criminal Code* have since changed.

"Cold cases" usually become the subject of a new or revived investigation owing to technological advances in investigative techniques that allow for additional evidence to be obtained — for example, DNA analysis of bodily fluids. Most commonly, these cases involve sexual offences and murder.

While there is a limitation period of six months from the time of the alleged offence for prosecuting summary conviction offences (generally minor offences), proceedings for many offences under the *Criminal Code* may be commenced at any time. (These include both indictable offences and offences for which proceedings may be by summary conviction or by indictment, called "hybrid offences".) Allegations of criminal conduct that took place more than 30 years ago can become the source of an investigation leading to charges.

For example, where an act of sexual intercourse took place without consent and the female complainant was not the wife of the accused man, today the accused would be charged with an offence of sexual assault. Before the shift in thinking in Canadian criminal law in the early 1980s, which led to the amalgamation of the sexual offences against adults, the charge would have been one of rape contrary to s. 143 of the *Criminal Code*.

It is the offence that existed at the time of the alleged occurrence that is to be the subject of the charge. Therefore, it is essential to find the relevant provision in the version of the *Criminal Code* applicable at that time, and to examine the wording. This is the wording you need to draft the charge correctly.

The easiest method for finding the relevant provision is to locate, at the library, three old annual Criminal Codes such as Martin's (which has been published annually since 1955). These three editions should be: one published in the year in which the offence allegedly occurred; one published in the preceding year; and one published in the following year.

It is advisable to check all three volumes, so that you are aware of any amendments that may have been passed around the time of the alleged offence. If there are any amendments, you will need to examine the dates of the amendments to establish exactly which version of the provision applied on the date of the alleged offence.

What section should you look up? The Concordance may be able to provide you with an answer. If you are still unable to find it, look up the subject (*e.g.*, theft) in the Index of the edition you are searching.

 Exercise

5.3 A rape case from January 1973 is re-investigated and a DNA match is discovered. Can the current sexual assault provisions be used in the information?

_____

_____

_____

_____

_____

_____

LEGISLATIVE AMENDMENT HISTORY

More information regarding legislative changes is available in each section of the *Criminal Code* itself. At the end of each section, you will see a reference to one or more enactments. These legislative references provide a legislative history of the particular section.

A list of all these references, including every amending enactment made to the *Criminal Code* since R.S.C. 1985, c. C-46, can also be found on the five pages preceding s. 1 of the *Criminal Code* (CC/1 to CC/5). Using this information, you can determine the precise date on which the section came into force.

Similar information is also provided for the related statutes such as the *Controlled Drugs and Substances Act* and the *Canada Evidence Act*. All amendments for the statute are listed at the beginning, and information is also provided at the end of each section to which amendments have been made.

Example 5.6

Turn to s. 786, Application of Part / Limitation (reproduced below). At the end of the section, you will see two legislative references. The first is "R.S., c. C-34, 721", and it is a duplication of the information found in the Concordance.

APPLICATION OF PART / Limitation.

786. (1) Except where otherwise provided by law, this Part applies to proceedings as defined in this Part.

(2) No proceedings shall be instituted more than six months after the time when the subject-matter of the proceedings arose, unless the prosecutor and the defendant so agree. R.S., c. C-34, 721; 1997, c. 18, s. 110.

Example 5.6 Legislative history: Martin's 2005 edition

The second reference is "1997, c. 18, s. 110". If you look up s. 786 in Martin's 1996 edition (reproduced below) and compare subsec. (2) with the current version, you will see that in the 1996 edition the words "unless the prosecutor and the defendant so agree" are not a part of subsec. (2). This second reference in the current Code provides a citation for the 1997 amendment that made this change to subsec. (2).

APPLICATION OF PART / Limitation.

786. (1) Except where otherwise provided by law, this Part applies to proceedings as defined in this Part.

(2) No proceedings shall be instituted more than six months after the time when the subject-matter of the proceedings arose. R.S., c. C-34, 721.

Example 5.6 Legislative history: Martin's 1996 edition

Example 5.7

Look at the list of amendments on page CC/4 (reproduced on page 42). At the 10th line from the top, the entry begins, "Amended 1997, c. 18, ss. 1 to 115; s. 107.1 in force May 2, 1997". When you match this information with the reference following subsec. 786(2) (in the 2005 edition), you understand that the change in the procedural law expressed in subsec. 786(2) (s. 110 of the amending statute) became effective on May 2, 1997.

Follow these systematic steps each time you need to track legislative changes and learn the date on which an amendment took effect.

Example 5.7
Legislative history:
list of amendments

MARTIN'S CRIMINAL CODE, 2005

Amended 1996, c. 16, s. 60(1)(*d*); brought into force July 12, 1996 by SI/96-67
Amended 1996, c. 19, ss. 65 to 76; brought into force May 14, 1997 by SI/97-47, *Can. Gaz.,*
    Part II, May 14, 1997 (but see ss. 61 to 63)
Amended 1996, c. 31, ss. 67 to 72; brought into force January 31, 1997 by SI/97-21, *Can.*
    Gaz., Part II, February 5, 1997
Amended 1996, c. 34, s. 1 (see ss. 3 to 8); to come into force by order of the Governor in
    Council
Amended 1997, c. 16, s. 2; brought into force May 26, 1997 by SI/97-66
Amended 1997, c. 17, ss. 1 to 10; brought into force August 1, 1997
Amended 1997, c. 18, ss. 1 to 115; s. 107.1 in force May 2, 1997; ss. 1, 23, 27 to 39, 99, 100
    and 109 in force May 14, 1997; ss. 2 to 22, 24 to 26, 40 to 98, 101 to 107, 108 and 110 to
    115 in force June 16, 1997, all by SI/97-62, *Can. Gaz., Part II*, May 28, 1997
Amended 1997, c. 23, ss. 1 to 20 and 26; ss. 1 to 20 in force May 2, 1997; s. 26 brought into
    force December 1, 1998

Exercises

5.4 Can you determine on what date conduct generally described as "Disarming a Peace Officer" became a specifically defined substantive criminal offence?

_____

_____

_____

_____

_____

_____

5.5 Look up the amending Act 2002, c. 13, on the list of amendments preceding the *Criminal Code*. Different portions of the amending Act, numbered chapter 13, came into force on different dates. On what date did s. 11 come into force?

_____

_____

_____

_____

_____

_____

Shaded Text

INTRODUCTION

Shaded text is used throughout Martin's to indicate clearly to the reader that this text is not a section of the statute like the others. Generally, the shading is used to identify an amendment of the statute that is *not yet in force* or to identify a *regulation*. It may also be used to signify an "Editor's Note". On closer examination of the shaded text, the reason for it should be evident.

AMENDMENTS

Provisions that are amendments but not yet brought into force at the date of printing of Martin's are displayed in a shaded box. If you are working with such a provision, it will be necessary to do further research to determine whether it has been brought into force since the publication of Martin's. You can check this most easily by looking at the Department of Justice Web site at http://laws.justice.gc.ca/en/ or telephoning the Department of Justice at 1-800-622-6232 for more information.

 Example 6.1

In the 2005 edition of Martin's, there is a Note in a shaded box in s. 117.07 of the *Criminal Code* (reproduced on page 44) that indicates an amendment to paragraph 117.07(2)(g). This amendment was not in force at the date of printing of the 2005 edition of Martin's. If the shading is gone from subsequent editions, this means that the Governor in Council has since ordered it into force. If the shading remains, it will be necessary to look at the Department of Justice Web site or to telephone the department (see the end of the previous paragraph for details).

REGULATIONS

Regulations are rules made by government administrators under the authority of a statute. They can be changed more quickly than statutory provisions since the legislative process is bypassed. Regulations generally fill in the details needed to properly administer and enforce a statute.

Martin's includes, for the reader's convenience, certain regulations made under the authority of the *Firearms Act*, S.C. 1994-95, c. 39, which are important in the interpretation of two sections of the *Criminal Code* (subsec. 84(1) and s. 117.07). These regulations are inserted after the commentary following each of the sections, and shading is used to set them apart from the rest of the text.

PUBLIC OFFICERS / Definition of "public officer".

117.07. (1) Notwithstanding any other provision of this Act, but subject to section 117.1, no public officer is guilty of an offence under this Act or the *Firearms Act* by reason only that the public officer

(*a*) possesses a firearm, a prohibited weapon, a restricted weapon, a prohibited device, any prohibited ammunition or an explosive substance in the course of or for the purpose of the public officer's duties or employment;

(*b*) manufactures or transfers, or offers to manufacture or transfer, a firearm, a prohibited weapon, a restricted weapon, a prohibited device, any ammunition or any prohibited ammunition in the course of the public officer's duties or employment;

(*c*) exports or imports a firearm, a prohibited weapon, a restricted weapon, a prohibited device or any prohibited ammunition in the course of the public officer's duties or employment;

(*d*) exports or imports a component or part designed exclusively for use in the manufacture of or assembly into an automatic firearm in the course of the public officer's duties or employment;

(*e*) in the course of the public officer's duties or employment, alters a firearm so that it is capable of, or manufactures or assembles any firearm with intent to produce a firearm that is capable of, discharging projectiles in rapid succession during one pressure of the trigger;

(*f*) fails to report the loss, theft or finding of any firearm, prohibited weapon, restricted weapon, prohibited device, ammunition, prohibited ammunition or explosive substance that occurs in the course of the public officer's duties or employment or the destruction of any such thing in the course of the public officer's duties or employment; or

(*g*) alters a serial number on a firearm in the course of the public officer's duties or employment.

(2) In this section, "public officer" means

(*a*) a peace officer;

(*b*) a member of the Canadian Forces or of the armed forces of a state other than Canada who is attached or seconded to any of the Canadian forces;

(*c*) an operator of a museum established by the Chief of the Defence Staff or a person employed in any such museum;

(*d*) a member of a cadet organization under the control and supervision of the Canadian Forces;

(*e*) a person training to become a police officer or a peace officer under the control and supervision of
   (i) a police force, or
   (ii) a police academy or similar institution designated by the Attorney General of Canada or the lieutenant governor in council of a province;

(*f*) a member of a visiting force, within the meaning of section 2 of the *Visiting Forces Act*, who is authorized under paragraph 14(*a*) of that Act to possess and carry explosives, ammunition and firearms;

(*g*) a person, or member of a class of persons, employed in the public service of Canada or by the government of a province or municipality who is prescribed to be a public officer; or

Note: Para. 117.07(2)(*g*) amended by the following 2003, c. 22, s. 224(*z*.23) (to come into force by order of the Governor in Council):

(*g*) a person, or member of a class of persons, employed in the federal public administration or by the government of a province or municipality who is prescribed to be a public officer; or

(*h*) the Commissioner of Firearms, the Registrar, a chief firearms officer, any firearms officer and any person designated under section 100 of the *Firearms Act*. 1995, c. 39, s. 139; 2003, c. 8, s. 7.

Example 6.1
An amendment that is not yet in force

Example 6.2

Following s. 117.07, Public Officers, are the *Firearms Act* Regulations Prescribing Public Officers (reproduced below). Subsection (2) of these Regulations states that they came into force on December 1, 1998.

SYNOPSIS

This section acts as an exception to liability otherwise triggered by the offences under the Code or the *Firearms Act*. Subsections (1) and (2) exempt wide categories of law enforcement and armed forces personnel acting in the course of their duties or employment.

REGULATIONS PRESCRIBING PUBLIC OFFICERS

1. (1) A member of any of the following classes of persons, if employed in the public service of Canada or by the government of a province or municipality, is a public officer for the purposes of paragraph 117.07(2)(*g*) of the *Criminal Code*:

    (*a*) employees who are responsible for the examination, inventory, storage, maintenance or transportation of court exhibits and evidence;

    (*b*) employees of police forces or other public service agencies who are responsible for the acquisition, examination, inventory, storage, maintenance, issuance or transportation of firearms, prohibited weapons, restricted weapons, prohibited devices, prohibited ammunition or explosive substances;

    (*c*) technicians, laboratory analysts and scientists who work at forensic or research laboratories;

    (*d*) armourers and firearms instructors who work at police academies or similar institutions designated under subparagraph 117.07(2)(*e*)(ii) of the *Criminal Code*, or are employed by a federal or provincial department of natural resources, fisheries, wildlife, conservation or the environment, or by Revenue Canada;

    (*e*) park wardens and other employees of a federal or provincial department who are responsible for the enforcement of laws and regulations dealing with natural resources, fisheries, wildlife, conservation or the environment;

    (*f*) immigration officers;

    (*g*) security personnel employed by the Security Service of the House of Commons or by the Senate Protective Service within the Parliamentary Precinct; and

    (*h*) aircraft pilots employed by the Department of Transport or other public service agencies.

(2) For the purposes of subsection (1), the expression "public service agencies" has the same meaning as in section 1 of the Public Agents Firearms Regulations.

Coming into Force

2. These Regulations come into force on December 1, 1998. **SOR/98-466; SOR/98-472.**

**Example 6.2
Regulations under
the *Firearms Act***

EDITOR'S NOTE

Occasionally the authors and editors of Martin's have provided additional information about a subject raised in Martin's that they thought would be useful to readers. A shaded box with the heading "Editor's Note" presents this additional explanation.

Example 6.3

There is an Editor's Note on the first page of the *Controlled Drugs and Substances Act* (reproduced on page 46). This note explains the content, structure and historical context of this legislation, which was enacted in 1996 as a replacement for older statutes dealing with the regulation of certain dangerous drugs and narcotics.

CONTROLLED DRUGS AND SUBSTANCES ACT

1996, Chap. 19, ss. 1 to 60 (but see ss. 61 to 63); brought into force May 14, 1997 by SI/97-47, *Can. Gaz.*, *Part II*, May 14, 1997

Amended 1996, c. 8, s. 35; brought into force July 12, 1996 by SI/96-69, *Can. Gaz., Part II,* July 24, 1997

Amended 1996, c. 19, s. 93.2; brought into force May 14, 1997 by SI/97-47, *Can. Gaz., Part II,* May 14, 1997

Amended SOR/97-230, *Can. Gaz., Part II,* May 14, 1997

Amended 1997, c. 18, s. 140; brought into force May 14, 1997 by SI/97-62.

Amended SOR/98-157, *Can. Gaz., Part II,* March 12, 1998

Amended SOR/98-173, *Can. Gaz., Part II,* March 19, 1998

Amended 1999, c. 5, ss. 48 and 49; brought into force May 1, 1999 by para. (*b*) of SI/99-24

Amended SOR/99-371, *Can. Gaz., Part II,* September 29, 1999

Amended SOR/99-421, *Can. Gaz., Part II,* October 21, 1999

Amended SOR/2000-220, *Can. Gaz., Part II,* June 1, 2000; in force September 1, 2000 as provided by s. 3

Amended 2001, c. 32, ss. 47 to 56, in force January 7, 2002 by para. (*a*) of SI/2002-17

**Example 6.3
Editor's explanation
of the content,
structure and
historical context
of this statute**

Editor's Note: The *Controlled Drugs and Substances Act* creates a new scheme for the regulation of certain dangerous drugs and narcotics, now known as "controlled substances". The Act replaces the *Narcotic Control Act*, R.S.C. 1985, c. N-1 and Part III [Controlled Drugs] and Part IV [Restricted Drugs] of the *Food and Drugs Act*, R.S.C. 1985, c. F-27. The essential scheme of the legislation is similar to the former *Narcotic Control Act* and the *Food and Drugs Act*.

Schedules / An important part of the legislation is the schedules to the Act: Schedule I – includes the most dangerous drugs and narcotics, such as phencyclidine, heroin and cocaine. Schedule II – lists cannabis and its derivatives. Schedule III – includes many of the more dangerous drugs which previously were included in schedules G and H to the *Food and Drugs Act*, such as the amphetamines and lysergic acid diethylamide (LSD). Schedule IV – includes many of the drugs formerly included in Schedule G to the *Food and Drugs Act*. These drugs, such as the barbiturates, while dangerous, have therapeutic uses. As was the case under Part III of the *Food and Drugs Act*, simple possession of Schedule IV drugs is not an offence.

Possession / Under s. 4(1), simple possession of any of the drugs and narcotics listed in Schedules I, II and III of the *Controlled Drugs and Substances Act* is an offence unless the person is authorized to be in possession by the regulations. The offence under s. 4(1) is a Crown option offence. The penalty for breach of s. 4(1) depends upon the Schedule in which the substance is included. In addition, a special penalty scheme has been included for possession of small quantities of Schedule II [cannabis] offences. Where the subject matter of the offence is a Schedule II substance in an amount that does not exceed the amount set out in Schedule VIII, then the accused is guilty only of a summary conviction offence and the maximum penalty is a $1,000 fine and/or six months' jail. Further, even where the amounts exceed the Schedule VIII amounts and the Crown proceeds by indictment, the offence is within the absolute jurisdiction of the provincial court where the substance is listed in Schedule II.

"Double-doctoring" / Under s. 4(2), it is an offence to seek or obtain any of the scheduled substances from a practitioner, such as a physician, without disclosing particulars relating to the acquisition of any of the scheduled substances within the preceding 30 days. This is the so-called "double-doctoring" offence which was found in both the *Food and Drugs Act* and

CD / 1

7 Table of Cases

The Table of Cases lists alphabetically all the cases included in Martin's, with complete citations for each case. To the right of the case citation, there is a column listing the section number(s) of the *Criminal Code* or other statute(s) where you will find a reference to the case (in the Annotations section of the commentary).

Because judgments often deal with more than one issue, case Annotations may cover several issues. Sometimes the same case will be annotated under two or more sections of the *Criminal Code* and/or other statutes.

If, when you are researching an issue, you recall the case name but not where the annotation is to be found in Martin's, the Table of Cases will assist you.

Example 7.1

Look in the Table of Cases for the case name *Duong, R. v.* (reproduced below). There are two different cases under this name. The first one, decided in 1998, lists three section references: "23, 657.2, (CE)23". These references tell you that the decision in the 1998 case of *R. v. Duong* relates to the interpretation of ss. 23 and 657.2 of the *Criminal Code* and s. 23 of the *Canada Evidence Act*.

Dunn, R. v. (1975), 28 C.C.C. (2d) 538, 33 C.R.N.S. 299 (Co. Ct.) 183
Dunn, R. v. (1977), 36 C.C.C. (2d) 495, 38 C.R.N.S. 383 (C.A.), affd [1979] 2
    S.C.R. 1012 *sub nom*. R. v. Yee; R. v. Ross, 52 C.C.C. (2d) 127........................ 189
Dunn, R. v. (1980), 8 M.V.R. 198 (B.C.C.A.) 254
Dunn, R. v., [1982] 2 S.C.R. 677, 1 C.C.C. (3d) 1 .... (CD)2
Dunn, R. v., [1995] 1 S.C.R. 226, 95 C.C.C. (3d) 289 .... (CH)11
Dunnett, R. v. (1990), 62 C.C.C. (3d) 14, 111 N.B.R. (2d) 67 (C.A.), leave to
    appeal to S.C.C. refused 62 C.C.C. (3d) vi, 116 N.B.R. (2d) 450*n*...................... 254
Dunning, R. v. (1979), 50 C.C.C. (2d) 296 (Ont. C.A.) 10
Duong, R. v. (1998), 124 C.C.C. (3d) 392, 15 C.R. (5th) 209 (C.A.)................23, 657.2,
                                      (CE)23
Duong, R. v. (2002), 162 C.C.C. (3d) 242, 49 C.R. (5th) 165 (B.C.C.A.), leave
    to appeal to S.C.C. refused 167 C.C.C. (3d) vi.................................. 529.3
Dupont, R. v. (1976), 22 N.R. at p. 519 (Alta. S.C. App. Div.), affd [1978] 1
    S.C.R. 1017, 11 A.R. 148.. 444

Example 7.1
Section references
for a case

Turn to s. 23 of the *Criminal Code*. Under the Annotations heading, in the second paragraph after the heading "Elements of offence" (reproduced below), you will find the reference to *R. v. Duong* (1998), 124 C.C.C. (3d) 392, 15 C.R. (5th) 209 (Ont. C.A.).

Example 7.1
Discussion of case in the Annotations for s. 23 of the Code

ANNOTATIONS

Elements of offence – Mere failure to disclose the fact that an offence has been committed in his presence does not make the accused an accessory after the fact: *R. v. Dumont* (1921), 37 C.C.C. 166, 64 D.L.R. 128 (Ont. C.A.); nor does the mere failure to aid in the apprehension of the principal: *R. v. Young* (1950), 98 C.C.C. 195, 10 C.R. 142 (Que. C.A.).

The charge must allege the commission of a specific offence and the Crown must prove that the alleged accessory knew that the person assisted was a party to that offence. This burden will be met if it is proven that the accused had actual knowledge of the offence committed or actual suspicion combined with a conscious decision not to make inquiries which could confirm that suspicion. Where the accused chooses to make no inquiries, speculation as to what the accused would have learned if the inquiries had been made is irrelevant to the determination of the blameworthiness of that accused's state of mind: *R. v. Duong* (1998), 124 C.C.C. (3d) 392, 15 C.R. (5th) 209 (Ont. C.A.).

Next turn to s. 657.2 of the *Criminal Code*, and then s. 23 of the *Canada Evidence Act*. Under the Annotations for these sections (reproduced below), you will again find references to the 1998 case of *R. v. Duong*.

Example 7.1
Discussion of case in the Annotations for s. 657.2 of the Code

ANNOTATIONS

Even aside from subsec. (2), the principal's conviction is admissible on the accessory's trial as evidence that the principal committed the crime. This rule does not offend Charter notions of fairness. The rule does not place any persuasive or even evidentiary burden on the accused to disprove a fact in issue. It also does not foreclose a full exploration of the principal's guilt on the trial of the accessory. Finally, the fact that the principal was appealing his conviction did not render evidence of that conviction inadmissible at the accessory's trial. However, in the circumstances it was appropriate to adjourn the accessory's appeal to await the outcome of the principal's appeal: *R. v. Duong* (1998), 124 C.C.C. (3d) 392, 15 C.R. (5th) 209 (Ont. C.A.). *Contra*: *R. v. Hamel* (1993), 20 C.R. (4th) 68, [1993] R.J.Q. 999 (C.A.).

ANNOTATIONS

A judge who grants an authorization to intercept private communications does so as a judge of the court not as a *persona designata* and a certified copy of the authorization is therefore admissible under this section: *R. v. Cordes*, [1979] 1 S.C.R. 1062, 47 C.C.C. (2d) 46, 10 C.R. (3d) 186 (7:0).

On the trial of a charge of being an accessory after the fact, a certified copy of the indictment endorsed by the trial judge and indicating that the principal offender had been convicted was admissible under this section to prove the conviction of the principal offender: *R. v. Duong* (1998), 124 C.C.C. (3d) 392, 15 C.R. (5th) 209 (Ont. C.A.).

Example 7.1
Discussion of case in the Annotations for s. 23 of the *Canada Evidence Act*

As we have seen in the case of *R. v. Duong*, the Table of Cases may list more than one case under the name or initials that you are looking up. How do you know which case is the one you need to read about for your research?

Example 7.2

You want to find information about a case named *Archer*, which you think dealt with weapons and was decided in the early 1980s. When you look for *Archer* in the Table of Cases (reproduced below), you find five cases by that name. A quick examination narrows your search to two cases decided in the early 1980s. Notice that one case is listed for ss. 84 and 91, contained in Part III / Firearms and Other Weapons; you have narrowed your search further. Using the citation, you can locate the reference you are looking for.

Appleby, R. v. (1974), 21 C.C.C. (2d) 282, 10 N.B.R. (2d) 162 (C.A.)....................830
Aranda, R. v. (1992), 69 C.C.C. (3d) 420, 6 O.R. (3d) 776 (Gen. Div.) 187
Arason, R. v. (1992), 78 C.C.C. (3d) 1, 37 W.A.C. 20 (B.C.C.A.) ....(CD)5
Araujo, R. v., [2000] 2 S.C.R. 992, 149 C.C.C. (3d) 449 (S.C.C.) 185, 186, 487, 676
Archer, R. v. (1972), 26 C.R.N.S. 225 (Ont. C.A.) 650
Archer, R. v. (1981), 59 C.C.C. (2d) 384, 21 C.R. (3d) 352 (Ont. C.A.)....................522
Archer, R. v. (1983), 6 C.C.C. (3d) 129 (Ont. C.A.) 84, 91
Archer, R. v. (1989), 47 C.C.C. (3d) 567, 65 Alta. L.R. (2d) 183 (C.A.) .... 487, (CE)37
Archer, R. v. (1989), 47 C.C.C. (3d) 567, 94 A.R. 323 (C.A.) ....(CE)37.1
Arcuri, R. v., [2001] 2 S.C.R. 828, 157 C.C.C. (3d) 21 ....541, 548
Argentina (Republic) v. Mellion, [1987] 1 S.C.R. 536, 33 C.C.C. (3d) 334............ (CH)7
Arkell, R. v., [1990] 2 S.C.R. 695, 59 C.C.C. (3d) 65 ....231, (CH)7
Armstrong v. Wisconsin (1972), 7 C.C.C. (2d) 331, [1972] 3 O.R. 229 (H.C.J) 537

**Example 7.2
Different cases listed
under the same name**

When a case is appealed, its name does not change. Sometimes cases with the same name are the same case, at different court levels. It may be necessary to read the lower court judgment as well as the appeal judgment. This will provide a fuller picture of the facts of the case, which are usually detailed at length in the trial judgment. Most important, reading of the lower court judgment may be necessary because in many cases there are multiple legal issues, and not all legal determinations of the trial judge will be appealed. The trial level decisions and reasons may continue to stand on some issues in the case.

Exercises

7.1 Look up *Phillips v. Nova Scotia (Commission of Inquiry into the Westray Mine Tragedy)* in the Table of Cases. Which section of which statute should you refer to for information about this case?

_____

_____

_____

_____

_____

7.2 You are researching how quickly an investigating officer must administer a breathalyzer and your professor mentioned the *Carter* case. You look up *Carter* in the Table of Cases and discover there are several. How can you identify the case you want?

_____

_____

_____

_____

_____

7.3 What section of the *Criminal Code* relates to delay in administering breathalyzers?

_____

_____

7.4 Which of the *Carter* cases are about delay in administering breathalyzers?

_____

_____

_____

_____

_____

_____

_____

_____

_____

_____

_____

_____

Forms

INTRODUCTION

The final Part of the *Criminal Code*, Part XXVIII / Miscellaneous, sets out the structure of the forms to be used in criminal proceedings. Although subsec. 849(1) does permit some flexibility in the structure of the forms by specifying that "forms . . . varied to suit the case, or forms to the like effect are deemed to be good, valid and sufficient . . .", for practical purposes, the forms most often used are those provided in Part XXVIII.

The *Youth Criminal Justice Act* (reproduced in Martin's) came into force in April 2003, replacing the *Young Offenders Act*. Section 155 of the *Youth Criminal Justice Act* authorizes the Governor in Council to make regulations prescribing forms to be used for purposes of the new Act. When these new forms are available, they will be reproduced in Martin's. Note that by provision of subsec. 154(2) of the *Youth Criminal Justice Act*, the forms established by Part XXVIII of the *Criminal Code* may be used in the meantime.

WORKING WITH FORMS

If you look at any of the forms authorized under Part XXVIII of the *Criminal Code*, immediately below the form number, in parentheses (round brackets), you will find a reference to the section(s) or subsection(s) to which the form is applicable.

 Example 8.1

Look at Form 5.2 (reproduced on page 52), at the line immediately below the Form number. You will see the reference to s. 489.1. For information concerning the use of this form, look at s. 489.1 (reproduced on page 53).

Under subsecs. (1) and (2) of s. 489.1, a person who has seized any item in the course of a search must deal with the items in a specified manner and must do so "as soon as is practicable". Subsection (3) then requires that a report to a justice under s. 489.1 must be made using Form 5.2, "varied to suit the case", and must include, "in the case of a report in respect of a warrant issued by telephone or other means of telecommunication, the statements referred to in subsection 487.1(9)".

Example 8.1
The section to which this form applies

FORM 5.2

(Section 489.1)

Report to a Justice

Canada,
Province of ....,
(territorial division).

To the justice who issued a warrant to the undersigned pursuant to section 256, 487 or 487.1 of the *Criminal Code (or another justice for the same territorial division or, if no warrant was issued, any justice having jurisdiction in respect of the matter)*.

I, *(name of the peace officer or other person)* have *(state here whether you have acted under a warrant issued pursuant to section 256, 487 or 487.1 of the Criminal Code or under section 489 of the Criminal Code or otherwise in the execution of duties under the Criminal Code or other Act of Parliament to be specified)*

1. searched the premises situated at ....; and

2. seized the following things and dealt with them as follows:

Property Seized *(describe each thing seized)*	Disposition *(state, in respect of each thing seized, whether*
	(a) it was returned to the person lawfully entitled to its possession, in which case the receipt therefor shall be attached hereto, or
	(b) it is being detained to be dealt with according to law, and the location and manner in which, or where applicable, the person by whom it is being detained).

---

1. ....
2. ....
3. ....
4. ....

In the case of a warrant issued by telephone or other means of telecommunication, the statements referred to in subsection 487.1(9) of the *Criminal Code* shall be specified in the report.

Dated this .... day of .... A.D. ...., at ....

....
Signature of peace officer
or other person

R.S.C. 1985, c. 27 (1st Supp.), s. 184(3); R.S.C. 1985, c. 1 (4th Supp.), s. 17.

RESTITUTION OF PROPERTY OR REPORT BY PEACE OFFICER / Idem / Form.

489.1 (1) Subject to this or any other Act of Parliament, where a peace officer has seized anything under a warrant issued under this Act or under section 487.11 or 489 or otherwise in the execution of duties under this or any other Act of Parliament, the peace officer shall, as soon as is practicable,

    (*a*) where the peace officer is satisfied,

        (i) that there is no dispute as to who is lawfully entitled to possession of the thing seized, and

        (ii) that the continued detention of the thing seized is not required for the purposes of any investigation or a preliminary inquiry, trial or other proceeding,

    return the thing seized, on being issued a receipt therefor, to the person lawfully entitled to its possession and report to the justice who issued the warrant or some other justice for the same territorial division or, if no warrant was issued, a justice having jurisdiction in respect of the matter, that he has done so; or

    (*b*) where the peace officer is not satisfied as described in subparagraphs (*a*)(i) and (ii),

        (i) bring the thing seized before the justice referred to in paragraph (*a*), or

        (ii) report to the justice that he has seized the thing and is detaining it or causing it to be detained

    to be dealt with by the justice in accordance with subsection 490(1).

(2) Subject to this or any other Act of Parliament, where a person, other than a peace officer, has seized anything under a warrant issued under this Act or under section 487.11 or 489 or otherwise in the execution of duties under this or any other Act of Parliament, that person shall, as soon as is practicable,

    (*a*) bring the thing seized before the justice who issued the warrant or some other justice for the same territorial division or, if no warrant was issued, before a justice having jurisdiction in respect of the matter, or

    (*a*) report to the justice referred to in paragraph (*a*) that he has seized the thing and is detaining it or causing it to be detained,

to be dealt with by the justice in accordance with subsection 490(1).

(3) A report to a justice under this section shall be in the form set out as Form 5.2 in Part XXVIII, varied to suit the case and shall include, in the case of a report in respect of a warrant issued by telephone or other means of telecommunication, the statements referred to in subsection 487.1(9). R.S.C. 1985, c. 27 (1st Supp.), s. 72; 1993, c. 40, s. 17; 1997, c. 18, s. 49.

**Example 8.1
The form that relates
to this section**

As demonstrated above, having the relevant section(s) referred to with each form provides the user with much more information than is available from the form alone.

Exercises

8.1 Look up Form 7.1, Warrant to Enter Dwelling House. What section of the *Criminal Code* is referenced?

_____

_____

_____

8.2 Look up Form 6, Summons to a person charged with an offence. What sections of the *Criminal Code* are referenced?

_____

_____

_____

_____

_____

8.3 Look up Form 2, Information. What is this form used for?

_____

_____

_____

_____

_____

_____

_____

Offence Grid

INTRODUCTION

The Offence Grid, located near the end of the book and immediately before the Index, consists of over 25 pages numbered with the abbreviation "OG".

The Offence Grid is a chart that sets out procedural and sentencing information for each substantive offence created by the *Criminal Code* (not other statutes). Its purpose is to allow readers to quickly and easily determine whether a particular sentencing option or judicial order applies to an offence.

The first page of the Offence Grid (from Martin's 2005 edition) is reproduced on page 56.

The Offence Grid provides, at a glance, important information about offence sections of the Code. In particular, it shows:

- the type of offence (indictable, summary or hybrid);

- whether the trial of an offence lies within the absolute jurisdiction of the provincial court;

- maximum and minimum sentence;

- available sentencing options;

- illegal sentences; and

- judicial orders that you may wish to consider or that are mandatory.

Before using the Offence Grid, you should read the Caution and Note set out on pages OG/1 and OG/2.

TYPE OF OFFENCE

The *Criminal Code* classifies offences into three types: indictable, summary and hybrid. The classification of an offence determines the procedures for trial that are available to the Crown and the accused.

The first page of the Offence Grid

SECTION	TYPE	MAX./MIN. SENTENCE	DISCHARGE s. 730	SUSPENDED SENTENCE s. 731(1)(a)	FINE ALONE s. 734	FINE & PROBATION s. 731(1)(a)	PRISON ss. 718.3, 787	PRISON & PROBATION s. 731(1)(b)	PRISON & FINE s. 734	INTERMITTENT s. 732	FINE PROB. & INTERMIT s. 732	VICTIM SURCHARGE s. 737	CONDITIONAL SENTENCE s. 742.1	COMMENTS (applicability depends on circumstances of case)
57(1) Forge passport or use forged passport	Indictable	14 yrs	✗	✓	✓	✓	✓	✓	✓	✓	✓	✓		
57(2) Passport, false statement	Hyb-Ind.	2 yrs	✓	✓	✓	✓	✓	✓	✓	✓	✓	✓	✓	
	Hyb-Sum.	6 mth/2000*	✓	✓	✓	✓	✓	✓	✓	✓	✓	✓	✓	
57(3) Possession, forged passport	Indictable	5 yrs	✓	✓	✓	✓	✓	✓	✓	✓	✓	✓	✓	
58 Fraud, use of citizenship certificate	Indictable	2 yrs	✓	✓	✓	✓	✓	✓	✓	✓	✓	✓	✓	
65 Riot	Indictable	2 yrs	✓	✓	✓	✓	✓	✓	✓	✓	✓	✓	✓	
66 Unlawful assembly	Summary	6 mth/2000*	✓	✓	✓	✓	✓	✓	✓	✓	✓	✓	✓	
72, 73 Forcible entry	Hyb-Ind.	2 yrs	✓	✓	✓	✓	✓	✓	✓	✓	✓	✓	✓	
	Hyb-Sum.	6 mth/2000*	✓	✓	✓	✓	✓	✓	✓	✓	✓	✓	✓	S. 110 discretionary firearms order.
76 Hijacking	Indictable	Life	✗	✓	✓	✓	✓	✓	✓	✓	✓	✓	✓	P S. 109 mandatory firearms order.
77 Endanger aircraft	Indictable	Life	✗	✓	✓	✓	✓	✓	✓	✓	✓	✓	✓	P S. 109 mandatory firearms order.
78 Take weapon or explosive on board	Indictable	14 yrs	✗	✓	✓	✓	✓	✓	✓	✓	✓	✓	✓	S. 109 mandatory firearms order. S. 491 mandatory weapon forfeiture order.
80(a) Breach of duty of care, explosives, causing death	Indictable	Life	✗	✓	✓	✓	✓	✓	✓	✓	✓	✓	✓	S. 109 mandatory firearms order.
80(b) Breach of duty of care, explosives, causing harm	Indictable	14 yrs	✗	✓	✓	✓	✓	✓	✓	✓	✓	✓	✓	S. 109 mandatory firearms order.
81(1)(a) & (b) Explosives, intent to cause death or harm	Indictable	Life	✗	✓	✓	✓	✓	✓	✓	✓	✓	✓	✓	P S. 109 mandatory firearms order.
81(1)(c) & (d) Explosives, placing or making	Indictable	14 yrs	✗	✓	✓	✓	✓	✓	✓	✓	✓	✓	✓	P S. 109 mandatory firearms order.
82(1) Explosives, possession w/o lawful excuse	Indictable	5 yrs	✓	✓	✓	✓	✓	✓	✓	✓	✓	✓	✓	
82(2) Explosives, for benefit of criminal organization	Indictable	14 yrs	✗	✓	✓	✓	✓	✓	✓	✓	✓	✓	✓	s. 82.1 requires sentence to be consecutive to any other sentence.
83 Prize fight	Summary	6 mth/2000*	✓	✓	✓	✓	✓	✓	✓	✓	✓	✓	✓	S. 110 discretionary firearms order.

* $100,000 for organizations for summary conviction offence s. 735.

✓ Sentence Option	✗ Illegal Sentence

P = Primary designated offence
S = Secondary designated offence
[see note on p. OG/2]

OG / 3

Indictable Offences

Indictable offences are the most serious criminal offences. Some indictable offences (listed in s. 469 — for example, murder) may be tried only by a superior court of criminal jurisdiction (such as the provincial Court of Appeal or the Superior Court of Justice) with a jury. For most other indictable offences, the accused may elect the mode of trial, choosing between trial by a provincial court judge, by judge alone or by judge and jury. However, a number of specific offences fall within the absolute jurisdiction of a provincial court judge, and the accused is normally denied the election as to mode of trial. These "absolute jurisdiction" offences are listed in s. 553, reproduced below.

Section 553 offences are identified in the Offence Grid by the notation "Absolute PCJ" in bold print in the "Type" column.

ABSOLUTE JURISDICTION.

553. The jurisdiction of a provincial court judge, or in Nunavut, of a judge of the Nunavut Court of Justice, to try an accused is absolute and does not depend on the consent of the accused where the accused is charged in an information

(*a*) with
  (i) theft, other than theft of cattle,
  (ii) obtaining money or property by false pretences,
  (iii) unlawfully having in his possession any property or thing or any proceeds of any property or thing knowing that all or a part of the property or thing or of the proceeds was obtained by or derived directly or indirectly from the commission in Canada of an offence punishable by indictment or an act or omission anywhere that, if it had occurred in Canada, would have constituted an offence punishable by indictment,
  (iv) having, by deceit, falsehood or other fraudulent means, defrauded the public or any person, whether ascertained or not, of any property, money or valuable security, or
  (v) mischief under subsection 430(4),
  where the subject-matter of the offence is not a testamentary instrument and the alleged value of the subject-matter of the offence does not exceed five thousand dollars;

(*b*) with counselling or with a conspiracy or attempt to commit or with being an accessory after the fact to the commission of
  (i) any offence referred to in paragraph (*a*) in respect of the subject-matter and value thereof referred to in that paragraph, or
  (ii) any offence referred to in paragraph (*c*); or

(*c*) with an offence under
  (i) section 201 (keeping gaming or betting house),
  (ii) section 202 (betting, pool-selling, book-making, etc.),
  (iii) section 203 (placing bets),
  (iv) section 206 (lotteries and games of chance),
  (v) section 209 (cheating at play),
  (vi) section 210 (keeping common bawdy-house),
  (vii) [*Repealed*, 2000, c. 25, s. 4.]
  (viii) section 393 (fraud in relation to fares),
  (viii.1) section 811 (breach of recognizance),
  (ix) subsection 733.1(1) (failure to comply with probation order),
  (x) paragraph 4(4)(*a*) of the *Controlled Drugs and Substances Act*, or
  (xi) subsection 5(4) of the *Controlled Drugs and Substances Act*. R.S., c. C-34, s. 483; 1972, c. 13, s. 40; 1974-75-76, c. 93, s. 62; R.S.C. 1985, c. 27 (1st Supp.), s. 104; 1992, c. 1, s. 58; 1994, c. 44, s. 57; 1995, c. 22, s. 2; 1996, c. 19, s. 72; 1997, c. 18, s. 66; 1999, c. 3, s. 37; 2000, c. 25, s. 4.

"Absolute jurisdiction" offences listed in the Code

**Example 9.1
Indictable and
"absolute jurisdiction"
offences**

SECTION	TYPE	MAX/MIN SENTENCE	DISCHARGE s. 730	SUSPENDED SENTENCE s. 731	FINE ALONE s. 734	FINE & PROBATION s. 731(1)(a)	PRISON ss. 718.3, 787	PRISON & PROBATION s. 731(1)(b)	PRISON & FINE s. 734	INTERMITTENT s. 732	FINE PROB. & INTERMIT s. 732	VICTIM SURCHARGE s. 737	CONDITIONAL SENTENCE s. 742.1	COMMENTS (applicability depends on circumstances of case)
193.1 Disclosure of information, radio-based telephone communications	Indictable	2 yrs	✓	✓	✓	✓	✓	✓	✓	✓	✓	✓	✓	S. 194 discretionary order of punitive damages to maximum of $5,000 on application of person aggrieved.
201(1) Keeping gaming or betting house	Indictable **Absolute PCJ**	2 yrs	✓	✓	✓	✓	✓	✓	✓	✓	✓	✓	✓	S. 462.37 proceeds of crime forfeiture order on Crown application.
201(2) Person found in gaming or betting house or owner permitting use	Summary	6 mth/2000	✓	✓	✓	✓	✓	✓	✓	✓	✓	✓		
202 Betting, pool-selling, book-making, etc.	Indictable **Absolute PCJ**	1st offence: 2 yrs	✓	✓	✓	✓	✓	✓	✓	✓	✓	✓	✓	S. 462.37 proceeds of crime forfeiture order on Crown application. Higher penalty for second or subsequent offence requires compliance with s. 727.
		2nd offence: 14 days min., 2 yrs max.	x	x	x	x	✓	✓	✓	✓	✓	✓	x	
		3rd & subsq: 3 mth min., 2 yrs max.	x	x	x	x	✓	✓	✓	✓	✓	✓	x	
203 Placing bets on behalf of others	Indictable **Absolute PCJ**	1st offence: 2 yrs	✓	✓	✓	✓	✓	✓	✓	✓	✓	✓	✓	
		2nd offence: 14 days min., 2 yrs max.	x	x	x	x	✓	✓	✓	✓	✓	✓	x	
		3rd & subsq: 3 mth min., 2 yrs max.	x	x	x	x	✓	✓	✓	✓	✓	✓	x	
206(1) Lotteries and games of chance	Indictable **Absolute PCJ**	2 yrs	✓	✓	✓	✓	✓	✓	✓	✓	✓	✓	✓	
206(4) Buying, taking or receiving lot, ticket or other device	Summary	6 mth/ 2000*	✓	✓	✓	✓	✓	✓	✓	✓	✓	✓	✓	
210(1) Keep common bawdy house	Indictable **Absolute PCJ**	2 yrs	✓	✓	✓	✓	✓	✓	✓	✓	✓	✓	✓	S. 210(3) notice of conviction to be served on owner, landlord or lessor. S. 462.37 proceeds of crime forfeiture order on Crown application.
210(2) Inmate, etc. of common bawdy house	Summary	6 mth/ 2000*	✓	✓	✓	✓	✓	✓	✓	✓	✓	✓	✓	S. 462.37 proceeds of crime forfeiture order on Crown application.

Example 9.1

Look at the first offence listed in the Offence Grid on page OG/12 in Martin's 2005 edition (reproduced on page 58). In the first column, as you read from left to right, the section number for the offence is shown together with a description of the prohibited conduct the offence covers. In this example, s. 193.1, the description is "Disclosure of information, radio-based telephone communications".

In the next column to the right, the type of offence is identified. Here the type is "Indictable". Take a look at the second offence listed on the same page, subsec. 201(1), "Keeping gaming or betting house". Here too the type is "Indictable", but there is also the notation "Absolute PCJ" in bold print. Therefore, the Offence Grid tells you that for a s. 193.1 offence, the accused may elect the mode of trial, while for a subsec. 201(1) offence, the case must be tried before a provincial court judge.

Section 553 is also important in the context of arrest procedures. Paragraph 495(2)(*a*) of the *Criminal Code*, Arrest Without Warrant by Peace Officer, prohibits a peace officer from arresting without warrant for an indictable offence listed in s. 553 in certain specified circumstances.

This is essential information for police and other peace officers, since an arrest made without warrant outside the authority provided by the *Criminal Code* constitutes an unlawful arrest. An unlawful arrest is likely to trigger a Charter challenge at trial. This could jeopardize the prosecution of the case and even raise the possibility of a civil suit against the arresting officer and his or her employer.

Summary Conviction Offences

A summary conviction offence is a relatively minor criminal offence tried without a jury or preliminary inquiry. These offences are identified in the Offence Grid by the notation "Summary" in the "Type" column. An example is subsec. 201(2) on page OG/12, reproduced on page 58.

Hybrid Offences

Hybrid offences can be prosecuted either by indictment or by summary conviction procedure. The choice belongs to the Crown. However, a hybrid offence is deemed to be indictable unless and until the Crown elects to proceed by the summary conviction procedure. (This rule is found in para. 34(1)(*a*) of the *Interpretation Act*, R.S.C. 1985, c. I-21.)

Whether the Crown proceeds by indictment or by summary conviction procedure has important consequences for the accused. For example, as discussed above, in the case of an indictable offence, the accused may choose the mode of trial (with or without a preliminary inquiry/jury); in the case of a summary conviction offence, this choice is normally not available.

The Crown's election of proceedings for a hybrid offence also affects the maximum and minimum penalties to which the accused may be subject if convicted of the offence. These penalties are discussed below under the heading "Maximum/Minimum Sentence".

Example 9.2

Look at the entry for s. 88, "Possession for purpose dangerous to the public", on page OG/4 (reproduced below). In the "Type" column, you find the notations "Hyb-Ind." and "Hyb-Sum." These notations tell you that the Crown can choose to prosecute either by indictment or by summary procedure.

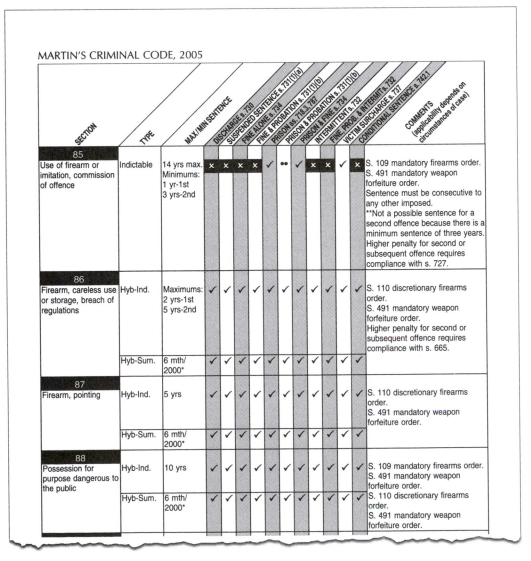

MARTIN'S CRIMINAL CODE, 2005

SECTION	TYPE	MAX/MIN SENTENCE	DISCHARGE s. 730	SUSPENDED SENTENCE s. 731(1)(a)	FINE ALONE s. 734	FINE & PROBATION s. 731(1)(b)	PRISON ss. 718.3, 787	PRISON & PROBATION s. 731(1)(b)	INTERMITTENT s. 732	FINE, PROB. & INTERMIT s. 734	VICTIM SURCHARGE s. 737	CONDITIONAL SENTENCE s. 742.1	COMMENTS (applicability depends on circumstances of case)
85 Use of firearm or imitation, commission of offence	Indictable	14 yrs max. Minimums: 1 yr-1st 3 yrs-2nd	x	x	x	x	✓	●●	✓	x	x	✓	x	S. 109 mandatory firearms order. S. 491 mandatory weapon forfeiture order. Sentence must be consecutive to any other imposed. **Not a possible sentence for a second offence because there is a minimum sentence of three years. Higher penalty for second or subsequent offence requires compliance with s. 727.
86 Firearm, careless use or storage, breach of regulations	Hyb-Ind.	Maximums: 2 yrs-1st 5 yrs-2nd	✓	✓	✓	✓	✓	✓	✓	✓	✓	✓	S. 110 discretionary firearms order. S. 491 mandatory weapon forfeiture order. Higher penalty for second or subsequent offence requires compliance with s. 665.
	Hyb-Sum.	6 mth/ 2000*	✓	✓	✓	✓	✓	✓	✓	✓	✓	✓	
87 Firearm, pointing	Hyb-Ind.	5 yrs	✓	✓	✓	✓	✓	✓	✓	✓	✓	✓	S. 110 discretionary firearms order. S. 491 mandatory weapon forfeiture order.
	Hyb-Sum.	6 mth/ 2000*	✓	✓	✓	✓	✓	✓	✓	✓	✓	✓	
88 Possession for purpose dangerous to the public	Hyb-Ind.	10 yrs	✓	✓	✓	✓	✓	✓	✓	✓	✓	✓	S. 109 mandatory firearms order. S. 491 mandatory weapon forfeiture order.
	Hyb-Sum.	6 mth/ 2000*	✓	✓	✓	✓	✓	✓	✓	✓	✓	✓	S. 110 discretionary firearms order. S. 491 mandatory weapon forfeiture order.

Example 9.2 Hybrid offence

9.1 What type of offence is "Theft over $5,000"? (If you are unsure of the section number, look it up in the Index.)

_____

_____

_____

9.2 What type of offence is "Theft $5,000 or less"?

_____

_____

_____

9.3 A suspect was observed by store security leaving a drugstore with toothpaste in her pocket, for which she had not paid. She was apprehended by the security officer as she walked out the door and the police were called. May the officer arriving on the scene arrest the suspect for "theft of $5,000 or less" without a warrant?

_____

_____

_____

_____

_____

_____

_____

_____

_____

_____

_____

_____

9.4 Would the answer to Exercise 9.3 differ if the suspect was not carrying identification?

_____

_____

_____

_____

_____

MAXIMUM/MINIMUM SENTENCE

The third column of the Offence Grid sets out the sentencing range. For most offences, there is no minimum sentence; therefore, only the maximum sentence is provided. Notable exceptions are the minimum sentences that apply to various weapons offences, certain offences resulting in death (such as murder) and a number of repeat offences.

In the case of hybrid offences, there may be a wide variation in the maximum sentences provided for indictable and summary proceedings. For example, for s. 88 (reproduced on page 60, below Example 9.2), for indictable proceedings the maximum sentence is imprisonment for 10 years, whereas for summary proceedings the maximum is merely 6 months' imprisonment and/or a fine of $2,000. This summary conviction penalty is the general penalty for summary conviction offences under s. 787 of the Code, and it applies in the majority of cases. For certain offences, however, the maximum term of imprisonment on summary conviction is extended to 18 months. These offences include assault causing bodily harm (s. 267), sexual assault (s. 271), forcible confinement (subsec. 279(2)) and failure to comply with a probation order (s. 733.1).

Note that where the maximum sentence for an offence is 5 years' imprisonment or a more severe punishment, the accused has the right to choose a trial by jury, as provided in para. 11(*f*) of the *Charter of Rights and Freedoms.*

SENTENCING OPTIONS

There are 11 columns to the right of the maximum/minimum sentence column, setting out the sentencing options for each offence. A check mark indicates that the particular sentencing option is available for the particular offence. Detailed information regarding the circumstances that may limit the applicability of each sentencing option is set out in the section(s) of the *Criminal Code* identified with each option.

Note that for most hybrid offences, there are no differences in the sentencing options for a particular offence whether the proceedings are by indictment or by summary conviction.

Discharge

Section 730, Conditional and Absolute Discharge, provides the court with sentencing options that allow the accused to avoid a criminal record. Pursuant to s. 6.1 of the *Criminal Records Act*, R.S.C. 1985, c. C-47, a person who receives a discharge for an offence does not have to apply for a pardon from the National Parole Board, but will have his or her record automatically destroyed. Clearly this is a sentencing option with a profound advantage for the accused.

The discharge is a sentencing option that occurs at the end of the trial where the accused is found guilty, or earlier if the accused pleads guilty. While it is necessary to enter a "conviction" on the record for some offences, for other, less serious offences, a conviction is discretionary and discharge is an option.

Example 9.3

Look at s. 57(1), "Forge passport or use forged passport" on the first page of the Offence Grid (reproduced on page 64). The "X" found in the black box in column 4 indicates that a discharge pursuant to s. 730 of the *Criminal Code* is not available, and consequently, the entry of a conviction on the record is mandatory. This is because s. 730 (reproduced on page 64) specifies that a discharge is not available as an option for offences for which a maximum punishment of 14 years' imprisonment or imprisonment for life may be imposed. (Clearly a discharge is also not available for an offence with a mandatory minimum sentence.)

Other Sentencing Options

The remaining columns each display another sentencing option, such as suspended sentence, fine alone and conditional sentence.

Example 9.4

Look at the column of the Offence Grid headed "Conditional sentence s. 742.1". When you look up s. 742.1 of the *Criminal Code* (reproduced on page 65), you will find that it sets out limitations on the availability of this option, which are related to the circumstances of both the offence and the offender.

When you use the Offence Grid to determine the sentencing options for a given offence, the check marks in the grid are only the first step. It is also necessary to refer to the applicable section for a particular option in order to understand the exact circumstances in which the option is available and when certain restrictions may apply.

OTHER COURT ORDERS

The last column of the Offence Grid, "Comments", lists additional discretionary and mandatory orders that the court may or must make. The section number for each kind of order is included in the column entries to direct you to more detailed information within the *Criminal Code*. It is important to read the section, since the applicability of judicial orders often depends significantly on the facts and circumstances of the particular case.

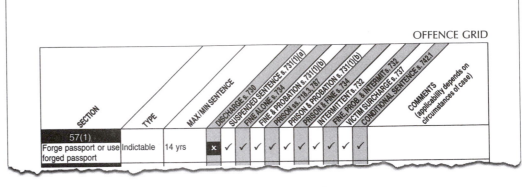

SECTION	TYPE	MAX./MIN. SENTENCE	DISCHARGE s. 730	SUSPENDED SENTENCE s. 731(1)(a)	FINE ALONE s. 734	FINE & PROBATION s. 731(1)(b)	PRISON ss. 718.3, 787	PRISON & PROBATION s. 731(1)(b)	PRISON & FINE s. 734	INTERMITTENT s. 732	FINE, PROB. & INTERMIT s. 732	VICTIM SURCHARGE s. 737	CONDITIONAL SENTENCE s. 742.1	COMMENTS (applicability depends on circumstances of case)
57(1) Forge passport or use forged passport	Indictable	14 yrs	✗	✓	✓	✓	✓	✓	✓	✓	✓	✓		

**Example 9.3
Discharge is not a
sentencing option**

**Example 9.3
Exclusion of
discharge as a
sentencing option**

Absolute and Conditional Discharges

CONDITIONAL AND ABSOLUTE DISCHARGE / Period for which appearance notice, etc., continues in force / Effect of discharge / Where person bound by probation order convicted of offence.

730. (1) Where an accused, other than an organization, pleads guilty to or is found guilty of an offence, other than an offence for which a minimum punishment is prescribed by law or an offence punishable by imprisonment for fourteen years or for life, the court before which the accused appears may, if it considers it to be in the best interests of the accused and not contrary to the public interest, instead of convicting the accused, by order direct that the accused be discharged absolutely or on the conditions prescribed in a probation order made under subsection 731(2).

(2) Subject to Part XVI, where an accused who has not been taken into custody or who has been released from custody under or by virtue of any provision of Part XVI pleads guilty of or is found guilty of an offence but is not convicted, the appearance notice, promise to appear, summons, undertaking or recognizance issued to or given or entered into by the accused continues in force, subject to its terms, until a disposition in respect of the accused is made under subsection (1) unless, at the time the accused pleads guilty or is found guilty, the court, judge or justice orders that the accused be taken into custody pending such a disposition.

(3) Where a court directs under subsection (1) that an offender be discharged of an offence, the offender shall be deemed not to have been convicted of the offence except that

    (*a*) the offender may appeal from the determination of guilt as if it were a conviction in respect of the offence;

    (*b*) the Attorney General and, in the case of summary conviction proceedings, the informant or the informant's agent may appeal from the decision of the court not to convict the offender of the offence as if that decision were a judgment or verdict of acquittal of the offence or a dismissal of the information against the offender; and

    (*c*) the offender may plead autrefois convict in respect of any subsequent charge relating to the offence.

(4) Where an offender who is bound by the conditions of a probation order made at a time when the offender was directed to be discharged under this section is convicted of an offence, including an offence under section 733.1, the court that made the probation order may, in addition to or in lieu of exercising its authority under subsection 732.2(5), at any time when it may take action under that subsection, revoke the discharge, convict the offender of the offence to which the discharge relates and impose any sentence that could have been imposed if the offender had been convicted at the time of discharge, and no appeal lies from a conviction under this subsection where an appeal was taken from the order directing that the offender be discharged. 1995, c. 22, s. 6; 1997, c. 18, ss. 107, 141; 2003, c. 21, s. 17.

OFFENCE GRID

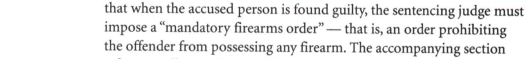

**Example 9.4
Sentencing option:
conditional sentence**

IMPOSING OF CONDITIONAL SENTENCE.

742.1 Where a person is convicted of an offence, except an offence that is punishable by a minimum term of imprisonment, and the court

(*a*) imposes a sentence of imprisonment of less than two years, and

(*b*) is satisfied that serving the sentence in the community would not endanger the safety of the community and would be consistent with the fundamental purpose and principles of sentencing set out in sections 718 to 718.2,

the court may, for the purpose of supervising the offender's behaviour in the community, order that the offender serve the sentence in the community, subject to the offender's complying with the conditions of a conditional sentence order made under section 742.3. 1995, c. 22, s. 6; 1997, c. 18, s. 107.1.

**Example 9.4
Limitations on
the availability of
a conditional
sentence as a
sentencing option**

Example 9.5

Look at the "Comments" column for s. 88, "Possession for purpose dangerous to the public" (reproduced on page 66). Reading across for proceedings by indictment, the first entry under "Comments" indicates that when the accused person is found guilty, the sentencing judge must impose a "mandatory firearms order" — that is, an order prohibiting the offender from possessing any firearm. The accompanying section reference tells you that the directive to impose that mandatory order is found in s. 109 of the *Criminal Code*.

Now look at proceedings by summary conviction. Here the sentencing judge has discretion to impose a firearms prohibition order or to choose not to do so. Section 110 of the *Criminal Code* is referenced, for examination of the foundation for such an order.

For both indictable and summary conviction offences, the court must issue an order requiring that the particular weapon that is the subject matter of the offence be forfeited to the Crown and be disposed of as the Attorney General directs. This mandatory order must be imposed upon a finding of guilt, as provided in s. 491 of the *Criminal Code*.

Accordingly, the police officer who examines the Offence Grid for this offence in s. 88, upon reading the "Comments" column, will know that the instructions about what to do with the weapon should be obtained from the local Crown Attorney, who is the agent of the provincial (or territorial) Attorney General.

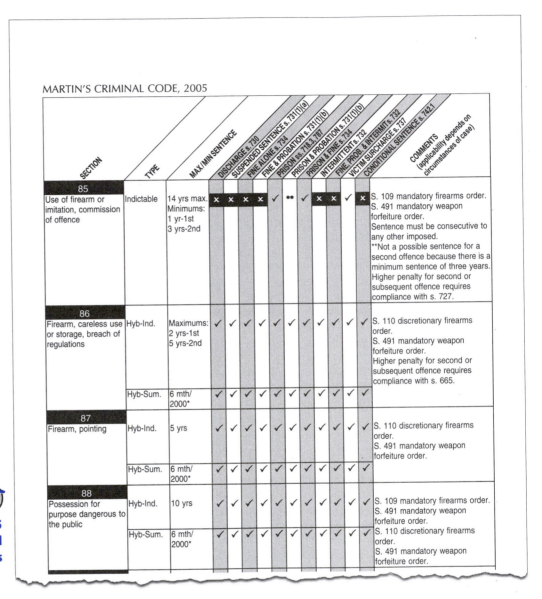

MARTIN'S CRIMINAL CODE, 2005

SECTION	TYPE	MAX/MIN SENTENCE	DISCHARGE s. 730	SUSPENDED SENTENCE s. 731(1)(a)	FINE ALONE s. 734	FINE & PROBATION s. 731(1)(a)	PRISON ss. 718.3, 787	PRISON & PROBATION s. 731(1)(b)	PRISON & FINE s. 734	INTERMITTENT s. 732	FINE, PROB. & INTERMIT s. 732	VICTIM SURCHARGE s. 737	CONDITIONAL SENTENCE s. 742.1	COMMENTS (applicability depends on circumstances of case)
85 Use of firearm or imitation, commission of offence	Indictable	14 yrs max. Minimums: 1 yr-1st 3 yrs-2nd	X	X	X	X	✓	••	✓	X	X	✓	X	S. 109 mandatory firearms order. S. 491 mandatory weapon forfeiture order. Sentence must be consecutive to any other imposed. **Not a possible sentence for a second offence because there is a minimum sentence of three years. Higher penalty for second or subsequent offence requires compliance with s. 727.
86 Firearm, careless use or storage, breach of regulations	Hyb-Ind.	Maximums: 2 yrs-1st 5 yrs-2nd	✓	✓	✓	✓	✓	✓	✓	✓	✓	✓	✓	S. 110 discretionary firearms order. S. 491 mandatory weapon forfeiture order. Higher penalty for second or subsequent offence requires compliance with s. 665.
	Hyb-Sum.	6 mth/ 2000*	✓	✓	✓	✓	✓	✓	✓	✓	✓	✓	✓	
87 Firearm, pointing	Hyb-Ind.	5 yrs	✓	✓	✓	✓	✓	✓	✓	✓	✓	✓	✓	S. 110 discretionary firearms order. S. 491 mandatory weapon forfeiture order.
	Hyb-Sum.	6 mth/ 2000*	✓	✓	✓	✓	✓	✓	✓	✓	✓	✓	✓	
88 Possession for purpose dangerous to the public	Hyb-Ind.	10 yrs	✓	✓	✓	✓	✓	✓	✓	✓	✓	✓	✓	S. 109 mandatory firearms order. S. 491 mandatory weapon forfeiture order.
	Hyb-Sum.	6 mth/ 2000*	✓	✓	✓	✓	✓	✓	✓	✓	✓	✓	✓	S. 110 discretionary firearms order. S. 491 mandatory weapon forfeiture order.

Example 9.5 Mandatory and discretionary orders

Example 9.6

Look at the entry in the Offence Grid for s. 271, "sexual assault" (reproduced on page 68).

It is a hybrid offence, but a hybrid with a twist. The maximum penalty for summary conviction proceedings is 18 months' imprisonment and/ or a fine of $2,000. As discussed earlier, there are only a few of these "enlarged" sentences for summary conviction. They apply to offences that cause physical or psychological harm to a person of such a serious nature as to warrant a substantial term of imprisonment, even when prosecuted summarily.

Because a significant penalty is available in this case, the Crown will often elect to proceed by way of summary conviction. The complainant benefits from having to testify only once, since no preliminary inquiry is available to the accused in summary proceedings. In addition, the complainant is spared the anxiety of having to testify in front of 12 strangers constituting a jury.

Generally, the full spectrum of sentencing options is available for hybrid offences, regardless of the procedural election, and this is the case for a s. 271 offence.

The "Comments" column provides information about a number of additional discretionary and mandatory orders. In the case of s. 271, these include the following:

- A firearms prohibition order.

- A private testimony order. (This order allows a complainant or witness to testify without having to look at the accused.)

- A publication ban.

- A weapon forfeiture order.

- Prohibition from attending certain public places or taking certain employment where the complainant is under 14 years of age. (This order is intended to keep pedophiles away from children.)

The final entry in the "Comments" column is the letter "P". As indicated by the legend at the bottom of the page, "P" stands for "primary designated offence", and "S" stands for "secondary designated offence". The legend directs you to the note on page OG/2, which discusses the authority to order the taking of samples of bodily substances from a person found guilty or convicted of specified offences, for the purpose of forensic DNA analysis. Both the primary and secondary designated offences are defined in s. 487.04 of the *Criminal Code*. The details of the orders are set out in ss. 487.051 and 487.052 of the *Criminal Code*.

Note that judicial orders are effective from the moment they are pronounced, according to s. 3.1 of the *Criminal Code*. The binding authority of an order is not dependent upon its having been reduced to writing.

SECTION	TYPE	MAX/MIN SENTENCE	DISCHARGE s. 730	SUSPENDED SENTENCE s. 731(1)(a)	FINE ALONE s. 734	FINE & PROBATION s. 731(1)(b)	PRISON ss. 718.3, 787	PRISON & PROBATION s. 731(1)(b)	PRISON & INTERMIT. s. 732	FINE, PROB. & INTERMIT. s. 732	VICTIM SURCHARGE s. 737	CONDITIONAL SENTENCE s. 742.1	COMMENTS (applicability depends on circumstances of case)
267 Assault causing bodily harm or with weapon	Hyb-Ind.	10 yrs	✓	✓	✓	✓	✓	✓	✓	✓	✓	✓	Indictable, s. 109 mandatory firearms order. Summary conviction, s. 110 discretionary firearms order. S. 491 mandatory weapon forfeiture order.
	Hyb-Sum.	18 mth/ 2000*	✓	✓	✓	✓	✓	✓	✓	✓	✓	✓	P
268 Aggravated assault	Indictable	14 yrs	✗	✓	✓	✓	✓	✓	✓	✓	✓	✓	S. 109 mandatory firearms order. S. 491 mandatory weapon forfeiture order. P
269 Unlawfully cause bodily harm	Hyb-Ind.	10 yrs	✓	✓	✓	✓	✓	✓	✓	✓	✓	✓	Indictable, s. 109 mandatory firearms order. Summary conviction, s. 110 discretionary firearms order. S. 491 mandatory weapon forfeiture order. May be convicted notwithstanding that charge.
	Hyb-Sum.	18 mth/ 2000*	✓	✓	✓	✓	✓	✓	✓	✓	✓	✓	P
269.1 Torture	Indictable	14 yrs	✗	✓	✓	✓	✓	✓	✓	✓	✓	✓	S. 109 mandatory firearms order. S. 491 mandatory weapon forfeiture order. S
270 Assault officer, resist arrest, etc.	Hyb-Ind.	5 yrs	✓	✓	✓	✓	✓	✓	✓	✓	✓	✓	S. 110 discretionary firearms order. S. 491 mandatory weapon forfeiture order.
	Hyb-Sum.	6 mth/ 2000*	✓	✓	✓	✓	✓	✓	✓	✓	✓	✓	S (s. 270(1)(a) only)
271 Sexual assault	Hyb-Ind.	10 yrs	✓	✓	✓	✓	✓	✓	✓	✓	✓	✓	Indictable, s. 109 mandatory firearms order; summary conviction, s. 110 discretionary firearms order. S. 486(2.1) private testimony order. S. 486(3) discretionary publication ban. S. 491 mandatory weapon forfeiture order. S. 161 Discretionary prohibition from attending certain public places or taking certain employment where complainant under 14 years. P
	Hyb-Sum.	18 mth/ 2000*	✓	✓	✓	✓	✓	✓	✓	✓	✓	✓	

Example 9.6 Section 271

---

* $100,000 for organizations for summary conviction offence s. 735. ✓ Sentence Option ✗ Illegal Sentence

P = Primary designated offence
S = Secondary designated offence
[see note on p. OG/2]

After you have worked through these examples, it should be clear that the Offence Grid is an excellent starting point for your understanding of offences under the *Criminal Code*. Further examination of the relevant sections of the Code, as well as the related Cross-References, Synopsis and Annotations, is a crucial second step.

 Exercises

9.5 What sentencing option is not available for breaking and entering a dwelling house?

_____

_____

9.6 Are there any mandatory weapons orders for this offence?

_____

_____

_____

_____

9.7 What is the meaning of "S" in the "Comments" column?

_____

_____

_____

_____

_____

_____

Appendix / Forms of Charges

INTRODUCTION

Suggested wording for charges is set out in the Appendix at the back of the book. The Appendix is printed on coloured paper to make it easier to find.

Charges are included for selected offences created by the *Criminal Code* and the *Controlled Drugs and Substances Act*. Only those offences most commonly dealt with by police officers are included. For other offences, and in all cases where the fact situation is complex, the Crown Attorney should be consulted.

INFORMATION

In Canada, the primary charging document is an information. The form used for an information is Form 2, which you looked at in Exercise 8.3. Form 2 (reproduced on page 72) is located in Part XXVIII / Miscellaneous of the *Criminal Code*. The charge wording set out for each offence in the Appendix can be plugged into Form 2 after "The informant says that", to create the document charging the offence — the information.

The information is the starting point for criminal prosecution proceedings and is of considerable importance. Any error in the wording of a charge may result in delay of the proceedings or, at worst, in the charge being declared a nullity. Knowing how to find and use accepted wording for charges is important for law enforcement officers. The Appendix sets out suggested wording that is accepted by the courts.

FORM 2

(Sections 506 and 788)

Information

Canada,

Province of ....,

(territorial division).

    This is the information of C.D., of ...., *(occupation)*, hereinafter called the informant.

    The informant says that (*if the informant has no personal knowledge state that he believes on reasonable grounds and state the offence.*)

Sworn before me this .... day of   ....
.... , A.D. ....,   *(Signature of Informant)*
at ....

....
A Justice of the Peace in and
   for ....

    Note: **The date of birth of the accused may be mentioned on the information or indictment.**

Where the wording of the charge is inserted

IMPORTANCE OF GETTING IT RIGHT

Because of the emphasis on personal liberty in Canadian social and political thinking, laws that impose criminal sanctions upon the person are strictly construed. As criminal law developed from its roots, which lie in English common law, a body of principles designed to protect the individual from arbitrary punishment emerged. General principles are that criminal laws must be clearly defined, must be consistent and must be made known (or at least accessible) to the public.

Following upon those basic principles, when an allegation is made accusing a person of having committed an offence, the accusation, in the form of the charge, must comply with the procedural law governing the charging process. This requirement is reflected in various sections of the *Criminal Code* (including s. 581, examined below) and in the *Canadian Charter of Rights and Freedoms* (for example, para. 11(*a*)). In essence, the principles come down to ensuring that the charge discloses sufficient information to the accused person so that the person will be able to identify the transaction or course of conduct alleged to have been criminal.

Therefore, the charge must at the very least specify all of the factors that constitute the offence alleged to have been committed. The reason for these requirements is to allow the accused to be able to fully answer the accusation and to defend himself or herself against the charge.

ELEMENTS OF THE OFFENCE AND LIABILITY/PUNISHMENT PROVISIONS

The *Criminal Code* addresses two aspects of each offence: the elements of the offence and the liability/punishment provisions. The elements of the offence are the actions and circumstances that create and define the offence. The liability/punishment provisions state that a person who commits the offence (as described in the elements) is "guilty of an offence" and set out the punishment.

 Example 10.1

Look at s. 175, Causing Disturbance ... (reproduced below).

Subsection 175(1) outlines the elements of the offence of causing disturbance and also includes the punishment at the end of the subsection, where it states "is guilty of an offence punishable on summary conviction".

CAUSING DISTURBANCE, INDECENT EXHIBITION, LOITERING, ETC. / Evidence of peace officer.

175. (1) Every one who

   (*a*) not being in a dwelling-house, causes a disturbance in or near a public place,

      (i) by fighting, screaming, shouting, swearing, singing or using insulting or obscene language,

      (ii) by being drunk, or

      (iii) by impeding or molesting other persons,

   (*b*) openly exposes or exhibits an indecent exhibition in a public place,

   (*c*) loiters in a public place and in any way obstructs persons who are in that place, or

   (*d*) disturbs the peace and quiet of the occupants of a dwelling-house by discharging firearms or by other disorderly conduct in a public place or who, not being an occupant of a dwelling-house comprised in a particular building or structure, disturbs the peace and quiet of the occupants of a dwelling-house comprised in the building or structure by discharging firearms or by other disorderly conduct in any part of a building or structure to which, at the time of such conduct, the occupants of two or more dwelling-houses comprised in the building or structure have access as of right or by invitation, express or implied,

is guilty of an offence punishable on summary conviction.

(2) In the absence of other evidence, or by way of corroboration of other evidence, a summary conviction court may infer from the evidence of a peace officer relating to the conduct of a person or persons, whether ascertained or not, that a disturbance described in paragraph (1)(*a*) or (*d*) or an obstruction described in paragraph (1)(*c*) was caused or occurred. R.S., c. C-34, s. 171; 1972, c. 13, s. 11; 1974-75-76, c. 93, s. 9; 1997, c. 18, s. 6.

Example 10.1 Elements of the offence

Punishment

In Example 10.1, the liability/punishment provision is found at the end of the subsection describing the elements of the offence. Sometimes the liability/punishment provisions are found in separate sections, as in the following example.

Example 10.2

Look at s. 322, Theft (reproduced below).

Section 322 outlines the elements of the offence of theft but does not deal with liability/punishment. The Cross-References for s. 322 state that the punishment for theft is set out in s. 334 (reproduced on page 75).

Example 10.2 Elements of the offence

Where to find the punishment provision

Theft

THEFT / Time when theft completed / Secrecy / Purpose of taking / Wild living creature.

322. (1) Every one commits theft who fraudulently and without colour of right takes, or fraudulently and without colour of right converts to his use or to the use of another person, anything whether animate or inanimate, with intent,

> **(a) to deprive, temporarily or absolutely, the owner of it, or a person who has a special property or interest in it, of the thing or of his property or interest in it;**
>
> **(b) to pledge it or deposit it as security;**
>
> **(c) to part with it under a condition with respect to its return that the person who parts with it may be unable to perform; or**
>
> **(d) to deal with it in such a manner that it cannot be restored in the condition in which it was at the time it was taken or converted.**

(2) A person commits theft when, with intent to steal anything, he moves it or causes it to move or to be moved, or begins to cause it to become movable.

(3) A taking or conversion of anything may be fraudulent notwithstanding that it is effected without secrecy or attempt at concealment.

(4) For the purposes of this Act, the question whether anything that is converted is taken for the purpose of conversion, or whether it is, at the time it is converted, in the lawful possession of the person who converts it is not material.

(5) For the purposes of this section, a person who has a wild living creature in captivity shall be deemed to have a special property or interest in it while it is in captivity and after it has escaped from captivity. R.S., c. C-34, s. 283.

CROSS-REFERENCES

The punishment for theft is set out in s. 334 and therefore see that section for cross-references respecting mode of trial and release pending trial as well as special procedural provisions. For notes on the defence of mistake generally, see notes under s. 19. Section 323 deals with special property or interest in the case of oyster beds. Also, note s. 588 which deems certain persons to have a property interest in property of which they have the management, control or custody. Section 583(b) deals with sufficiency of an indictment which fails to name the person who owns or has a special property or interest in property mentioned in the count. Sections 324 to 333 define other means by which theft may be committed. Offences resembling theft are set out in ss. 335 to 342. The related offence of false pretences is dealt with in ss. 361 to 363. Fraudulently obtaining food and lodging is an offence under s. 364. The general offence of fraud is contained in s. 380. The offence of secret commissions is set out in s. 426. The offence of possession of goods obtained by commission of an indictable offence is set out in ss. 354 and 355. The break and enter offences are dealt with in ss. 348 to 352. Robbery is dealt with in ss. 343 and 344. For notes on doctrine of recent possession, see s. 354.

PUNISHMENT FOR THEFT.

334. Except where otherwise provided by law, every one who commits theft

    (*a*) is guilty of an indictable offence and liable to imprisonment for a term not exceeding ten years, where the property stolen is a testamentary instrument or the value of what is stolen exceeds five thousand dollars; or

    (*b*) is guilty

        (i) of an indictable offence and is liable to imprisonment for a term not exceeding two years, or

        (ii) of an offence punishable on summary conviction,

    where the value of what is stolen does not exceed five thousand dollars. R.S., c. C-34, s. 294; 1972, c. 13, s. 23; 1974-75-76, c. 93, s. 25; R.S.C. 1985, c. 27 (1st Supp.), s. 43; 1994, c. 44, s. 20.

Example 10.2 Punishment for a s. 322 offence

It is the liability/punishment provision that declares the specific conduct to be an offence and that is referenced at the end of the charge, where it states "contrary *etc.*" If you have difficulty finding the liability/punishment section for a particular offence, turn to the Cross-References, the Index or the Offence Grid for assistance.

It is important to ensure that you have correctly identified the liability/punishment section so that it can be inserted in the information. Where the elements provision is in a separate section from the liability/punishment provision, it is a common error to insert the elements section instead. There is nothing wrong with using both sections, and many police officers choose to do so.

WHAT AN INFORMATION NEEDS

Rules for Drafting (S. 581)

Section 581, Substance of Offence, sets out the rules that govern the drafting of *Criminal Code* charges. The purpose of the rules is to ensure that the accused knows the charge and is able to defend himself or herself fully and fairly.

As explained in the Synopsis for s. 581, an information generally deals with a "single transaction" only. However, a "single transaction" may involve a series of events or a number of victims. Court interpretations of the "single transaction rule" can be found in the Annotations for this section.

Section 581 also provides that there are several permissible methods of stating the offence. The officer drafting the information may use (a) popular language; (b) words from the *Criminal Code* section that describes the offence; or (c) words sufficient to give the accused notice of the offence. Despite this flexibility, most charges are drafted using method (b), the words of the section that creates and describes the offence.

In addition to describing the legal elements of the offence, s. 581 requires that the information contain sufficient detail to allow the accused to identify the event leading to the charge or charges. Specifically, the information must set out the time, place and subject-matter of the alleged crime.

Missing Information (S. 583)

It may be permissible for certain information to be missing from the charge, provided that the absence of these details does not prevent the accused from exercising his or her right to a full and fair defence. Among these details, as listed in s. 583, Certain Omissions Not Grounds for Objection, are the victim's name, a precise description of the place and the means by which the alleged offence was committed.

Particulars (S. 587)

To address the lack of detail that may result from s. 583, and to ensure that the accused has enough information to make a defence, s. 587, What May Be Ordered, allows an accused person to apply to the court for further details (called "particulars") about the alleged crime. The court may then order the prosecutor to provide this additional information to the defence.

Multiple Accuseds and Charges

Although the draft charges contained in the Appendix all show a singular accused person, two or more individuals may be charged on the same information. The substantive wording of the draft charges in the Appendix is not changed, and the charge specifies that A.B. and X.Y. did commit the particular offence.

The information may also charge the accused with more than one offence. In this case, each separate charge is set out as a separate "count" and each count is numbered. Suppose, for example, that it is alleged that A.B. and X.Y. committed theft and they are also accused of mischief. Count 1 sets out the charge of theft — for example, "Count 1: A.B. and X.Y. on . . . at . . . did steal . . ." — followed by the words "and further that", followed by "Count 2: A.B. and X.Y. did commit mischief by. . . ."

HOW TO DRAFT AN INFORMATION CORRECTLY

To draft an information, you can complete Form 2 using the wording suggested in the Appendix and adding the specific details of the charge.

Turn to the Appendix at the back of Martin's and look up the section number for the offence that the accused has allegedly committed. Here you will find the suggested wording.

It is good practice also to locate the section in the *Criminal Code* and to read it carefully, to ensure that every essential element required to constitute the offence is included in the wording of the charge. It is the substantive section, which outlines the elements of the offence, that is used in this part of the charge. Remember, however, that it is the section number for the *liability/punishment* provision that is inserted at the end of the charge, after "contrary *etc.*"

The following examples illustrate how to complete the Form 2 information with correct wording for the charge.

 Example 10.3

Look at the first page of the listed forms of charges in the Appendix. The first entry is the offence created by para. 57(1)(*a*), "Forging a passport" (reproduced below). The wording in italics contained within square brackets "[*specify the forged passport*]" is a drafting instruction and not part of the wording of the charge itself. At the end of the charge, "*etc.*" is another drafting instruction, which will be replaced by a reference to the punishment provision.

FORMS OF CHARGES UNDER THE *CRIMINAL CODE*

57(1)(*a*) Forging a passport
  A.B. on .... at .... did forge a passport [*specify the forged passport*] contrary *etc.*

Example 10.3
Suggested wording
for the charge

If you take the wording for the charge and plug it into Form 2 with the details of the particular allegation, it should look like the following:

FORM 2

(*Sections 506 and 788*)

Information

Canada,

Province of Ontario,
(Whichever) Region.

   This is the information of Chuck Doright, peace officer, **hereinafter called the informant.**

   The informant says that he believes on reasonable grounds that Able Baker, on July 31, 2003, at the City of Wherever, did forge a passport, to wit: a Canadian passport bearing number 123456, showing a bearer name of Rich Roundtrip, contrary to section 57(1)(a) of the *Criminal Code*.

   Sworn before me this [*etc.*]

Example 10.4

Look at the second offence listed in the Appendix, created by para. 57(1)(*b*), "Uttering a forged passport" (reproduced below).

Example 10.4
Suggested wording
for the charge

57(1)(*b*) Uttering a forged passport
A.B. on .... at .... did knowingly

(i) use [*or* deal with *or* act upon] a forged passport to wit [*specify the forged passport*] as if it were genuine contrary *etc.*

or

(ii) cause [*or* attempt to cause] C.D. to use [*or* deal with *or* act upon] a forged passport to wit [*specify the forged document*] as if it were genuine contrary *etc.*

The wording contained in the first set of square brackets has both italics and normal type. The italicized "*or*" is instructional, whereas the normal type is a part of the substantive allegation. Consequently, the substantive charge for using the forged passport would read as follows:

> Able Baker, on July 31, 2003, at the City of Wherever, did knowingly use a forged passport, to wit: a Canadian passport bearing number 123456, showing a bearer name of Rich Roundtrip, as if it were genuine contrary to section 57(1)(b)(i) of the *Criminal Code*.

Alternatively, the charge could read "did knowingly deal with [*etc.*]" or "did knowingly act on [*etc.*]". All of the suggested charges constitute a means by which the offence under subpara. 57(1)(*b*)(i) could be committed. From a practical standpoint, most Crown Attorneys would want to see the charge laid in the broadest way permissible in law. Because the offence created by subpara. 57(1)(*b*)(i) can be committed in any manner stated — that is, using, dealing with or acting on the forged passport — the information would probably be worded in this way:

> Able Baker, on July 31, 2003, at the City of Wherever, did knowingly use, deal with or act on a forged passport, to wit: a Canadian passport bearing number 123456, showing a bearer name of Rich Roundtrip, contrary to section 57(1)(b)(i) of the *Criminal Code*.

Therefore, although the italicized "*or*" is instructional, it may be included in the body of the charge for practical reasons. Offences that can be committed in alternative ways should be charged in the broadest terms because in many cases the alleged conduct allows for more than one criminal act to be identified.

10.1   The facts as gathered by a police officer are that Cecil Dry had his Mighty lawn mower (model number 22-D) stolen from his home in the City of Wherever by the accused Able Baker on July 31, 2004. Under what section would Mr. Baker be charged?

_____

_____

_____

_____

_____

_____

_____

_____

_____

_____

_____

10.2   What might the charge state?

_____

_____

_____

_____

_____

_____

_____

10.3   Compare this charge with the requirements set out in s. 581. Does it provide Mr. Baker with sufficient information to be able to identify the transaction and the offence?

_____

_____

_____

_____

_____

_____

_____

10.4 Where can you find all the elements of the offence of theft required before a charge can be properly laid?

_____

_____

_____

_____

_____

_____

_____

_____

10.5 Nowhere in the charge is there any information as to the manner in which Mr. Baker obtained Mr. Dry's lawn mower. Is this a problem?

_____

_____

_____

_____

_____

_____

_____

_____

_____

10.6 How can Mr. Baker find out how his dealings with this lawn mower, and with Mr. Dry, constitute an offence?

_____

_____

_____

_____

_____

_____

_____

10.7 There is a complaint from C.D. that her ex-boyfriend A.B. repeatedly communicated with her, against her wishes, between July 31, 2004 and August 29, 2004 in the City of Wherever, by sending flowers and cards and by telephoning and requesting reconciliation. This behaviour continued even though, at C.D.'s request, a police officer asked A.B. to stop. If the allegations can be proved, what section of the *Criminal Code* should you refer to, to find the elements of the offence?

_____

_____

_____

_____

_____

_____

_____

_____

_____

10.8 Look at the suggested wording (in the Appendix) immediately following s. 264(2)(*d*): "thereby causing C.D. to reasonably, in all the circumstances, fear for her safety . . . contrary *etc.*" Does this relate only to "engage in threatening conduct" as prohibited by s. 264(2)(*d*), or does it relate to one or more of the other paragraphs, such as s. 264(2)(*b*), as well?

_____

_____

_____

_____

_____

_____

_____

_____

_____

_____

10.9   How should the charge against A.B. be completed?

_____

_____

_____

_____

_____

_____

_____

_____

_____

_____

10.10   Why is s. 264(3) used instead of s. 264(2)(*b*)?

_____

_____

_____

_____

_____

_____

Index

The Index is topical and covers all statutes included in the book. Instead of page numbers, section numbers are used as references.

For sections of statutes other than the *Criminal Code*, abbreviations such as CH (the *Canadian Charter of Rights and Freedoms*) and YC (the *Youth Criminal Justice Act*) are used before the section reference. These abbreviations are the same as those used for page numbering, and they can be found listed in an editor's note at the top of page IN/1. Section numbers with no preceding initials are references to the *Criminal Code*.

General headings are capitalized and in bold type, and listed alphabetically. There are several levels of subheadings under most general headings. The Index is extensively cross-referenced to make it easy to find what you need even if you do not know the general heading to look under.

 Example 11.1

To find out the procedure required to obtain a telewarrant, turn to the page in the Index that shows the general heading "TELEWARRANTS" (reproduced on page 84). Instead of listing subheadings or providing a section number, the entry tells you to "*See*" two other general headings: "ARREST" and "SEARCH AND SEIZURE".

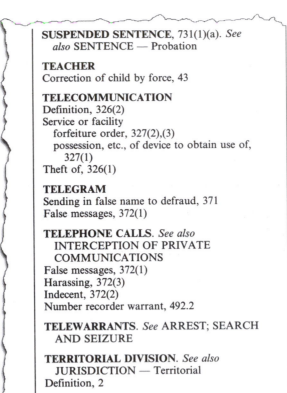

SUSPENDED SENTENCE, 731(1)(a). *See also* SENTENCE — Probation

TEACHER
Correction of child by force, 43

TELECOMMUNICATION
Definition, 326(2)
Service or facility
  forfeiture order, 327(2),(3)
  possession, etc., of device to obtain use of, 327(1)
Theft of, 326(1)

TELEGRAM
Sending in false name to defraud, 371
False messages, 372(1)

TELEPHONE CALLS. *See also* INTERCEPTION OF PRIVATE COMMUNICATIONS
False messages, 372(1)
Harassing, 372(3)
Indecent, 372(2)
Number recorder warrant, 492.2

TELEWARRANTS. *See* ARREST; SEARCH AND SEIZURE

TERRITORIAL DIVISION. *See also* JURISDICTION — Territorial
Definition, 2

TERRITORIAL JURISDICTION. *See also* JURISDICTION — Territorial
Arrest, search or seizure, and other powers, 477.3

**Example 11.1
Where to find
index entries for
information on
telewarrants**

If you look under "ARREST", you will find many subheadings, including "Warrant". Under "Warrant", there are again many entries, with section number references. Some may be of interest with respect to telewarrants. However, if you look under "SEARCH AND SEIZURE", you will find more subheadings, including "Telewarrants". Entries under this subheading include topics such as "formalities re warrant, 487.1(6)" and "proof of authorization, 487.1(11)", which are about procedures to be followed when obtaining a telewarrant. These references direct you to s. 487.1 of the *Criminal Code*, which you will need to examine closely.

Cross-References may also assist you if you look up a topic by a legal term no longer in use. For example, "bail" is no longer used in the *Criminal Code*. If you look up "BAIL" in the Index, you will be redirected to "JUDICIAL INTERIM RELEASE; RELEASE FROM CUSTODY".

Most of the section numbers referenced in the Index are in force. In some cases, however, references are included for sections that were not yet in effect, or were no longer in effect, when the Index was published. As Martin's notes at the beginning of the Index, such references are identified by printing of the section numbers in bold italic type.

11.1 What do you find when you look up the term "search warrant" in the Index?

_____

_____

_____

_____

11.2 You need to know what makes a search warrant "reasonable". Is there an entry for "reasonable search and seizure"? What are the references and where will you find them?

_____

_____

_____

_____

_____

_____

_____

12 Conclusion

After reading this guide and working through the examples and exercises, you should have a better understanding of what information lies within *Martin's Annual Criminal Code*, and of how you can access this information quickly and thoroughly.

Martin's is the first place to look when you are researching most criminal law issues. It provides basic research tools and a jumping-off point for more thorough investigation. Often you will find the answers to your questions in Martin's and will need to search no further.

13 Answers to Exercise Questions

1 Introduction to Martin's

(NOTE: There are no exercises in chapter 1.)

2 Table of Contents and Page Numbering

2.1 What is on page TC/1?

The first page of the Table of Cases.

2.2 What is on page C/1?

The first page of the Table of Contents.

2.3 What is on page YC/4?

The fourth page of the *Youth Criminal Justice Act*.

3 The Criminal Code

3.1 What Part of the *Criminal Code* deals with sexual offences?
(Hint: use the Table of Contents.)

Part V.

3.2 What section number is noted at the top corner of the first page
of the sexual offences Part?

Section 149 (in the 2005 edition of Martin's).

3.3 What is noted at the bottom corner?

> The page number.

3.4 When working with s. 177, Trespassing at Night, you will need to understand the meaning of "prowls by night". What is the definition of "night"?

> Section 2 defines "night" as "the period between nine o'clock in the afternoon and six o'clock in the forenoon of the following day". (Note that information about the meaning of "prowls" can be found in the Annotations for s. 177, and this is explained in Example 4.4.)

3.5 Where and how does the *Criminal Code* define "theft", "steal" and "robbery"? (Hint: use the Index.)

> Section 322 defines "theft" by specifying the elements of this offence. Section 2 states that "steal" means "to commit theft". Section 343 defines "robbery" by setting out the elements of this offence.

3.6 When working with s. 348, Breaking and Entering . . . , you will need to understand the meaning of "breaking", "entering" and "place". Where are the definitions for these terms? (Hint: use the Index.)

> Section 321 provides a definition of "break" that applies throughout Part IX / Offences Against Rights of Property. The meaning of entering is provided in s. 350, Entrance, and this definition applies to ss. 348 and 349. "Place" is defined in subsec. 348(3), and this definition applies to ss. 348 and 351.

4   Commentary: Cross-References, Synopsis and Annotations

4.1 Find the Cross-References under s. 253, Operating While Impaired. Where is "motor vehicle" defined? Where is "operate" defined? Where is the punishment set out?

> Section 2; s. 214; and s. 255.

4.2 Find the Cross-References for s. 175, Causing Disturbance. . . . What are a few of the related offences that an arresting officer should be aware of?

> Sections 63 to 69, "related to unlawful assembly"; s. 174, "public nudity"; s. 179, "vagrancy"; s. 180, "common nuisance"; and others.

4.3 Read s. 179, Vagrancy / Punishment, carefully and then try to write your own Synopsis. Compare it with the Synopsis provided in Martin's. Did you interpret the wording in a similar way? After reading the Martin's Synopsis, is your understanding of the section improved? Would it have been easier to understand the section if you had read the Martin's Synopsis first?

(NOTE: There are no right or wrong answers.)

4.4 Choose and read any section of the *Criminal Code*. Then read the Synopsis and the Cross-References. Was it beneficial to have read the Synopsis before the Cross-References? Choose and read another section, and then read the Cross-References before the Synopsis. Is there a particular order that works better for you?

(NOTE: There are no right or wrong answers.)

4.5 Is there likely to be a conviction under s. 175, Causing Disturbance . . . , where an accused gets into a loud swearing match with a friend in a secluded laneway? How about if there are passersby?

Proof of disturbance requires that someone was affected or disturbed, as held in *R. v. V.B. (J.G.)* (2002), 165 C.C.C. (3d) 494 (N.S.C.A.). If there was no one present to be bothered, a conviction is unlikely. If there were passersby who may have been disturbed, a conviction is more likely.

4.6 Paragraph (*d*) of s. 343, Robbery, provides that one commits robbery who "steals . . . while armed with an offensive weapon or imitation thereof". Where the accused holds up his hand with his first finger pointing forward and thumb up, imitating a gun, could he be convicted under para. 343(*d*)?

In the decision of *R. v. Gouchie* (1976), 33 C.C.C. (2d) 120 (Que. Sess. Peace), the court held that no part of the body can resemble an offensive weapon. If this ruling is followed, a conviction is unlikely.

4.7 Subparagraph 1(*a*)(iii) of s. 175, Causing Disturbance . . . , provides that everyone who causes a disturbance in or near a public place (not in a dwelling-house), by "impeding or molesting" others, has committed the offence. Has it become easier or more difficult to convict on this charge since 1980? (Hint: look at the Annotations for para. 175(1)(*a*).)

It has become easier. The lower court decision in *R. v. Goddard* (1971), 4 C.C.C. (2d) 396 (H.C.J.), in which proof of an affray, riot or unlawful assembly was required for conviction, was overruled by the Ontario Court of Appeal in *R. v. Berry* (1980), 56 C.C.C. (2d) 99. *Berry* held that "disturbance" was to be given its ordinary dictionary meaning.

4.8 The Quebec case of *R. v. Gouchie* (1976), 33 C.C.C. (2d) 120 (Que. Sess. Peace), referenced in the Annotations for s. 343, Robbery, was decided by a lower court. Is there another case that might be more persuasive in arguing that a hand gesture does not constitute an imitation of an offensive weapon?

> In the case of *R. v. Sloan* (1974), 19 C.C.C. (2d) 190, the British Columbia Court of Appeal held that to be "armed" means to possess an instrument. This case is binding on lower courts in British Columbia, unless and until it is overruled by the Supreme Court of Canada. It may be more persuasive than the *Gouchie* case in provinces other than Quebec. As these cases are consistent in their rulings, they would likely both be used by defence counsel.

5 Criminal Code Concordance

5.1 Look up the current s. 487, Information for Search Warrant, in the Concordance. What was the number of this section before the 1985 Revised Statutes of Canada were published?

> Section 443.

5.2 Did para. 487(1)(*c*.1), which allows for the search of "any offence-related property", exist in 1985 when the last Revised Statutes of Canada were published?

> No. This paragraph was enacted in 1997, as indicated in the square brackets "[en. 1997, c. 23, s. 12]".

5.3 A rape case from January 1973 is re-investigated and a DNA match is discovered. Can the current sexual assault provisions be used in the information?

> No. It is necessary to look up the old provisions that were in force in January 1973. The elements of the offence as they applied at the time of the offence must be included in the information.

5.4 Can you determine on what date conduct generally described as "Disarming a Peace Officer" became a specifically defined substantive criminal offence?

> The legislative reference for the section that creates the offence, s. 270.1, is "2002, c. 13, s. 11". This indicates that it was section 11 of the amending statute in 2002, numbered chapter 13, that enacted the offence.

5.5 Look up the amending Act 2002, c. 13, on the list of amendments preceding the *Criminal Code*. Different portions of the amending Act, numbered chapter 13, came into force on different dates. On what date did s. 11 come into force?

> Section 11 is not included with the listed sections for which coming into force was delayed; therefore, the date on which the offence became law was July 23, 2002.

6 Shaded Text

> (NOTE: There are no exercises in chapter 6.)

7 Table of Cases

7.1 Look up *Phillips v. Nova Scotia (Commission of Inquiry into the Westray Mine Tragedy)* in the Table of Cases. Which section of which statute should you refer to for information about this case?

> Section 579 of the *Criminal Code*. Note that this is a section number, not a page number. As there are several pages of Annotations for that section, it is necessary to search for the case on those pages.

7.2 You are researching how quickly an investigating officer must administer a breathalyzer and your professor mentioned the *Carter* case. You look up *Carter* in the Table of Cases and discover there are several. How can you identify the case you want?

> Look up "breathalyzer" in the Index to determine the relevant section number. Match this section number with the cases listed under *Carter* in the Table of Cases.

7.3 What section of the *Criminal Code* relates to delay in administering breathalyzers?

> Section 258 relates to the admissibility of breathalyzer results.

7.4 Which of the *Carter* cases are about delay in administering breathalyzers?

> The Table of Cases lists three *Carter* decisions as relevant to s. 258. Several points of law are covered in the Annotations for s. 258. The heading most closely related to the research topic is "Time element / as soon as practicable and within two hours", and two *Carter* decisions are cited — the 1980 British Columbia Court of Appeal case and the 1981 Saskatchewan Court of Appeal judgment. The third *Carter* case, heard by the Ontario Court of Appeal in 1985, can be found under a different heading — "Evidence to the contrary / expert evidence" — and is about a different point of law.

8 Forms

8.1 Look up Form 7.1, Warrant to Enter Dwelling House. What section of the *Criminal Code* is referenced?

> Section 529.1, Warrant to Enter Dwelling House.

8.2 Look up Form 6, Summons to a person charged with an offence. What sections of the *Criminal Code* are referenced?

> Section 493, definition of "summons"; s. 508, Justice to Hear Informant and Witnesses; and s. 512, Certain Actions Not to Preclude Issue of Warrant.

8.3 Look up Form 2, Information. What is this form used for?

> This form is used for laying charges. Specifically, s. 506 provides that an information laid under s. 504 or s. 505 may be in Form 2. Section 788 provides that summary proceedings must be commenced by laying an information in Form 2.

9 Offence Grid

9.1 What type of offence is "Theft over $5,000"? (If you are unsure of the section number, look it up in the Index.)

> Paragraph 334(*a*) provides that theft over $5,000 is an indictable offence.

9.2 What type of offence is "Theft $5,000 or less"?

Paragraph 334(*b*) identifies theft of $5,000 or less as a hybrid offence.

9.3 A suspect was observed by store security leaving a drugstore with toothpaste in her pocket, for which she had not paid. She was apprehended by the security officer as she walked out the door and the police were called. May the officer arriving on the scene arrest the suspect for "theft of $5,000 or less" without a warrant?

Generally no, as provided in s. 495, Arrest Without Warrant by Peace Officer. The Offence Grid indicates that "Theft $5,000 or less" is a hybrid offence, and where the Crown elects to proceed by indictment, it is an "Absolute PCJ" offence. Subsection 495(2) provides that a warrant is required for (a) s. 553 absolute jurisdiction offences, (b) hybrid offences, and (c) summary conviction offences. Note that the exceptions to the general rule requiring a warrant are also set out in s. 495. While store security caught the suspect in the act of committing the offence, the police officer did not arrive until afterwards; therefore, the "caught in the act" exception in para. 495(1)(*b*) does not apply.

9.4 Would the answer to Exercise 9.3 differ if the suspect was not carrying identification?

It might. Subsection 495(2) provides that if, having regard to the fact that the identity of the suspect cannot be established, the officer has reasonable grounds to believe that she will fail to attend court, an arrest may be made.

9.5 What sentencing option is not available for breaking and entering a dwelling house?

Section 348: discharge is not an option.

9.6 Are there any mandatory weapons orders for this offence?

Yes. Section 109 mandatory firearms order and s. 491 mandatory weapon forfeiture order.

9.7 What is the meaning of "S" in the "Comments" column?

"S" in the "Comments" column indicates that the offence of breaking and entering a dwelling house is a "secondary designated offence" for the purpose of authorizing the taking of a sample for DNA analysis.

10 Appendix / Forms of Charges

10.1   The facts as gathered by a police officer are that Cecil Dry had his Mighty lawn mower (model number 22-D) stolen from his home in the City of Wherever by the accused Able Baker on July 31, 2004. Under what section would Mr. Baker be charged?

Section 334(*b*) is the charging section that declares theft of property valued at $5,000 or less to be an offence and sets out the punishment. The charging section is not the same as the section that sets out the elements of the offence of theft. See Exercise 10.4 below regarding the substantive section, which sets out the elements of the offence.

10.2   What might the charge state?

Able Baker, on July 31, 2004, at the City of Wherever, did steal a Mighty lawn mower, model number 22-D, the property of Cecil Dry, of a value not exceeding five thousand dollars, contrary to section 334(b) of the *Criminal Code.*

10.3   Compare this charge with the requirements set out in s. 581. Does it provide Mr. Baker with sufficient information to be able to identify the transaction and the offence?

Yes. The charge describes the alleged theft, including details of time, place and subject-matter, which, together with the reference to s. 334(*b*), is sufficient to give notice of the offence.

10.4   Where can you find all the elements of the offence of theft required before a charge can be properly laid?

The elements of theft are outlined in the substantive section, s. 322. This is not the charging section and therefore is not referred to at the end of the charge where it states "contrary *etc.*" Section 334(*b*) is the charging section for this offence.

10.5   Nowhere in the charge is there any information as to the manner in which Mr. Baker obtained Mr. Dry's lawn mower. Is this a problem?

Not necessarily. Section 583 provides that certain information, such the means by which the alleged offence was committed, may be missing from the charge. However, the absence of such details must not prevent the accused from exercising his or her right to a full and fair defence.

10.6 How can Mr. Baker find out how his dealings with this lawn mower, and with Mr. Dry, constitute an offence?

> Mr. Baker can apply to the court for particulars under s. 587. The court may then order the prosecutor to provide the additional information to the defence.

10.7 There is a complaint from C.D. that her ex-boyfriend A.B. repeatedly communicated with her, against her wishes, between July 31, 2004 and August 29, 2004 in the City of Wherever, by sending flowers and cards and by telephoning and requesting reconciliation. This behaviour continued even though, at C.D.'s request, a police officer asked A.B. to stop. If the allegations can be proved, what section of the *Criminal Code* should you refer to, to find the elements of the offence?

> Section 264(2)(*b*), Criminal Harassment, "repeatedly communicating".

10.8 Look at the suggested wording (in the Appendix) immediately following s. 264(2)(*d*): "thereby causing C.D. to reasonably, in all the circumstances, fear for her safety . . . contrary *etc.*" Does this relate only to "engage in threatening conduct" as prohibited by s. 264(2)(*d*), or does it relate to one or more of the other paragraphs, such as s. 264(2)(*b*), as well?

> Section 264 makes it clear that this element of the offence applies to all of paragraphs 264(2)(*a*) to (*d*). Whatever conduct described in s. 264(2) is alleged, it must cause the person to reasonably fear, *etc.*, for it to be prohibited under this subsection. Consequently, this phrase needs to be included to complete the draft charge above.

10.9 How should the charge against A.B. be completed?

> A.B. between July 31, 2004, and August 29, 2004, at the City of Wherever, knowing that C.D. is harassed, or being reckless as to whether C.D. is harassed, did, without lawful authority, repeatedly communicate directly or indirectly with C.D. thereby causing C.D. to reasonably, in all the circumstances, fear for her safety contrary to section 264(3) of the *Criminal Code*.

10.10 Why is s. 264(3) used instead of s. 264(2)(*b*)?

> Section 264(3) is the charging section that declares the conduct to be an offence and indicates the punishment.

11   Index

11.1   What do you find when you look up the term "search warrant" in the Index?

> Under "SEARCH WARRANT", there is a cross-reference to "SEARCH AND SEIZURE — Warrants".

11.2   You need to know what makes a search warrant "reasonable". Is there an entry for "reasonable search and seizure"? What are the references and where will you find them?

> Yes. The references are 487.01(3) and CH8. The first reference is to section 487.01(3) of the *Criminal Code*; the second is to section 8 of the *Canadian Charter of Rights and Freedoms.*

12   Conclusion

> (NOTE: There are no exercises in chapter 12.)